WHAT DO YOU KNOW ABOUT HUMAN HARVESTING?

An Investigation of the Alien-Reptilian
Presence on Earth

FREDERICK DODSON

ISBN: 9798861813532

1

We Are Under Hostile Occupation

I've read a lot of books on supernatural, extraterrestrial and subterranean Reptilians. I was 27 years young when I read *Children of the Matrix* by David Icke. I was a teenager when I read *Gods of Eden* by William Bramley. Later I read *Bloodline of the Gods* by Nick Redfern. I've read many more obscure than these. As intriguing as the books were, none of them satisfied me. They did not reveal or direct me toward *tangible proof* of the reality of reptilian beings, physical or supernatural. I'm a practical person.

If we are really under occupation by hostile aliens, that would have *practical* implications for daily life. Maybe not for you. Maybe you say "It doesn't change the bottom line. I'd still need to pay the rent and put food on the table. I'd still look for someone to share my life with". Or more likely, you're like me and if you were 100% certain we were under hostile occupation, you'd have a change of plans. You'd want to gather intel on the occupiers, then create a group to defeat or methods to transcend them. But if it's not true, then even just reading about them is a colossal waste of time.

We all have the civic responsibility to ask:

Is it true?

This book is my quest to put the topic to rest for myself. If "the reptilian agenda" is real, we-the-people must take appropriate action, not just post context-less mystery-videos of shapeshifting people online, not just sit, wonder and rant about it. And if it's not real, we must hold those accountable spreading lies. I wouldn't be satisfied living in a society where people can get rich and famous with lies.

The current situation is that hundreds of millions, if not Billions of people believe in an alien presence in one form or another. The governing bodies of the world simply ignore this fact. Imagine the same on a smaller scale:

You're living in a small village community of 100 people. 50 of them believe in aliens and 20 of them are convinced that evil aliens are abducting some of them. Yet the Government–a group of 10 elders– does not address the issue at all. Either half of the people in the village are mentally ill and require healthcare or they're right, in which case the community should study the phenomenon and act upon it. *The fact that neither is happening* actually points to the reality of alien presence and influence. Not addressing the elephant in the room is anti-social, inhumane, even anti-human. If the elders don't believe in aliens, don't they care that half of their community is delusional? And if they do, don't they care to share their knowledge and concerns?

I've also been concerned about how people are treated when they talk about an alien or evil presence on Earth. They have been mocked, jeered at, ridiculed, insulted, marginalized, disenfranchised and even deplatformed. I don't understand this kind of treatment, frankly. If you think that reptilian believers are mentally ill, then instead of mocking them, wouldn't you feel compassion? Wouldn't you want to help them get a grip on reality so that they can have a job, a relationship and participate in society? Why would you mock the mentally unstable?

But if there's any chance they are telling the truth, they deserve attention. Or, if you're not sure whether it's true, at the very least one could keep an open mind. This jeering and shaming of people who think differently has a very bad vibe to it. It's like saying those who dare have thoughts outside of mainstream media *feed* should be derided. It's dumb and obnoxious. The shame around offbeat topics is really a sign that some sort of suppression of knowledge is, in fact, happening.

Anti-social, inhumane and anti-human trends in society stirred me to write this book. It wasn't reptilians or aliens. I'm more interested in why so many things happen that nobody asked for. No sentient being would conduct Government Business the way we have. No loving being would build supermarkets the way they are. Our foods and pharmaceuticals are so toxic they have made generations of people more sick, obese and dumbed down than ever. The mainstream news programmed into the collective is daily lies. Then they tell us that none of it is lies and only those dumb "conspiracy theorists" think so. Elections in supposedly free and civilized countries are stolen in front of everyone's eyes and the audience is too apathetic and hypnotized to do anything about it.

Any aspect of society reveals an anti-human agenda. Take, for example, architecture 200 years ago and architecture today. Whoever is in charge doesn't like humans that much.

Not only on a grand scale but also on a smaller one, we have anti-human trends. Just a few weeks ago, I heard from a realtor about a local building developer who had threatened the mayor at gunpoint to build houses in a certain area. Permission was at first denied, but after the "developers" used violence and intimidation, permissions were granted. I had to ask several times if this were true and how it could be true in the U.S. I said "we have laws. That can't be true". But it was. We point at other countries being "cesspools of corruption", but we had better clean our own house before pointing fingers.

I believe there is a "reptilian agenda"—a malevolent hidden influence that is not operating in humanity's best interest. Sure, this hidden influence doesn't have to be "reptilian" in nature. It could be something else. But the ancient traditions across cultures said they were snakes, dragons and upright walking, humanoid-reptilians.

Even though I believe, I am not starting this work with a readymade answer. The purpose is to share with you my investigation, step by step. A mere "vague feeling" that it's true is not enough for me to act on. I want to know for sure. And if Reptilians do in fact live among us, I'd like to know for how long they have been here and the *extent* of their infiltration. I'd also like to learn of already existing groups, people and beings who might be opposing them.

The best attitude for investigation is an open mind *willing* to believe either.

Despite the dark implications of this book, I have good news to share with you: If the *Reptilian agenda* exists, they are not at a point where they openly show themselves. They are afraid of us. And if they are scared, it means we are more powerful than we have been conditioned to believe. Throughout my career, I have collected experiential proof that normal people are capable of reality creation through focusing attention, telepathy, psychic perception, remote influencing, precision-intuition, remote viewing, healing through laying hands and having access to higher realms. At the same time, there is evidence that the malevolent beings *do not have the same powers.* This is why they operate in the shadows. This is why their resources and funds are spent on degrading humankind and on causing conflict. A people left to their own, without outside manipulation, tend to prosper. They have no strife between young and old, man and woman, skin colors, etc. Whoever is socially engineering these conflicts has a deep understanding of the limitations of the human mind and exploits them to their benefit. But the human spirit is powerful and despite billions spent each year to program, influence and manipulate humans, they still have to keep their presence secret and we still have plenty of people who are awake, and making a positive impact.

My method of investigation is to read the books of other investigators, to see whether I can independently verify or disprove the things they are saying. I have not chosen the big, bestselling books for this, but the works of fairly unknown authors. There is a good reason for this: If "the reptilian agenda" is real, then big-media and that includes books selling by the Millions, is contaminated by reptilian programming. They don't have the power or resources to control every small publisher and independent author. Rather, they believe that if they exercise control of the largest publishing houses, it'll be enough to keep human minds in check. Sure enough, I've found that small-audience writers offer a much deeper and more authentic look at reptilians than the famous ones. That's not to say all famous people are "remote controlled". Sometimes someone slips past the gatekeepers to become well known.

I write this book while living north of Orlando, Florida, not far from a place called Lake Jessup. The lake is home to 13000 alligators. I am surrounded by more alligators than anywhere in the U.S. During a hurricane flooding in 2022, I saw them swimming in front of my house. Surely it's no coincidence that, while living in such an environment, I decide to write about Reptilians. I'm "tuned in" at this location.

The reptilian agenda provides the adventure of a lifetime. The potential to break free of slavery but not quite having discovered that potential yet is exhilarating. We are on the very edge, on the cusp of self-discovery. May this book be yet another step to freedom.

2

A Copper City In The Rwenzori Mountains

Many years ago I read a book titled *The Hidden History of Africa* by Zulu shaman Credo Mutwa, in which fascinating claims of an ancient subterranean copper city are made:

Before human beings were created on this planet, there had existed a very wise race of people known as the Imanyukela. These people had come from the constellation known to white people as Orion, and they had inhabited our earth for thousands and thousands of years. And that before they had left our earth to return once more to the sacred Spider constellation, they made a great excavation under the earth, beneath the Ruwensory Mountains- the Mountains of the Moon.

And deep in the bowels of Mother Earth, the Imanyukela built a city of copper buildings. A city with a wall of silver all around it. A city built at the huge mountain of pure crystal. The mountain of knowledge. The mountain from which all knowledge on earth comes. And a mountain to which all knowledge on earth ultimately returns. This old woman told me that her grandmother had told her this story while she was still a virgin of some fifteen years or so and undergoing initiation into the mysteries and the culture of the Bahutu people. The old woman went on to tell me that many generations ago, there came to the land of the Bahutu, a group of little yellow skinned men, who wore colorful robes and strange brightly colored hats. These men, she said, had come in search of the great city of knowledge which they had heard many, many years ago, stands in the earth under the Mountains of the Moon - the Ruwensory Mountains.

This story remained in my mind and was one of the many, many strange stories that I had heard during my long, long travels through Africa. And then much to my amazement, in the year 1975, there arrived at my home in Soweto, a friendly bright priest from Tibet. The priest's name was Akyong Rin Poche, whom ever today I still regard as a great friend of mine, a man who sparkles like a glass of precious champagne. He is a man, unlike most Tibetan monks whom I have met in my life, who looks at life through the mask of humour. He is a man who ever is smiling. A man whose every word is perfumed with humour. A man who laughs readily. A lovely and lively fellow human being. I was honoured to talk to this man in one of the huts that formed the museum village that I had built in Soweto, and Akyong Rin Poche nearly knocked me over by asking me a question that caught me totally by surprise, and which brought back memories of bygone years in a green and half-forgotten Central African country. "Do you know anything," he asked," About the city of copper, which is said to be somewhere in Central Africa?" For a few moments I was stricken dumb by astonishment. And then I replied," Yes, honourable Rin Poche. In the days I was travelling through the land of the Watutsi and the Bahutu, the land that was then known as Rwanda Urundi, I heard a story about this mysterious city, and I also heard that this city lies deep under ground - under the Mountains of the Moon." Akyong Rin Poche threw another surprise at my feet. He told me how in olden days a great Lama led a group of fellow monks on an expedition into Central Africa in search of this mysterious city, and that Lama and his followers were never heard from again. I was stunned, here was an African story being confirmed by a man from Tibet.

That's the story in a nutshell. I've read a lot of things that sound like tall tales in my long and wonderful life. I enjoy adventurous storytelling or the borderlands of fiction and non-fiction. This story prompted me to research, to see if I could find just the slightest shred of evidence for any of it. Is Mutwa giving an honest account?

Mutwa speaks of an extraterrestrial people who came to earth and built a city inside Rwenzori (also spelled Ruwenzori and Ruwensory), a mountain range in Uganda and Congo. He calls them the Imanyukela. I looked up this name to see if I could find it in African mythology. I had to dig a little deeper to find something, but in the book "African Mythology from A to Z" by Patricia Lynch, I found the entry "Imana", which was the name the Hutu and Tutsi of Central Africa use for the God that created all things. I recognize the meaning of the name from my book *Extraterrestrial Linguistics:* Man-Uk-Ela the men of God (Ela) from Uk (Ophiucus star constellation).

Mutwa says the copper city attracted the attention of Tibetan monks who travelled to Africa at different times in history to inquire about it. Perhaps they were following a report in their own ancient records. The Tibetans have no shortage of tales of subterranean cities. The visiting Tibetans were witnessed by the Bahutu people.

At the time I read Mutwa, in around 2005, the only thing I knew about the Hutu (Bahutu) and Tutsi (here called Watutsi), is what I learned from western media: These were the people that partook in the biggest mass-murdering spree in recent History in the 1995 Rwandan war.

Typing "Akong Rinpoche" into a search engine, the first thing I found is that he was murdered.

From an article titled *"The Life and Murder of Akong Rinpoche"*:

On the morning of Tuesday, October 8, the prominent Tibetan lama, doctor, and humanitarian Akong Rinpoche was stabbed to death in a residential community in Chengdu, Sichuan Province, along with his nephew and monk attendant. The tragic ending of his life reflected his lifelong commitment to tasks and ideals that, to a degree exceptional among Tibetan lamas in the West, were difficult, controversial, and far-reaching in their implications.

Source: https://tricycle.org/article/life-and-murder-akong-rinpoche/

Elsewhere in Credo Mutwa's book, we learn even stranger things about this copper city:

Jabulon, sir, is a very strange god. He is supposed to be the leader of the Chitauli. He is a god, to my great surprise, which I find certain groups of White people, especially, worshipping. We have known about Jabulon for many, many centuries, we Black people. But I am surprised that there are White people who worship this god, and these people, amongst them, are people whom many have blamed for all the things that have happened on this Earth, namely, the Freemason people. We believe that Jabulon is the leader of the Chitauli. He is the Old One. And one of his names, in the African language, sir, is Umbaba-Samahongo - "the lord king, the great father of the terrible eyes" - because we believe that Jabulon has got one eye which, if he opens it, you die if he looks at you. It is said, sir, the Umbaba ran away from an eastern land during a power struggle with one of his sons, and he took refuge in Central Africa, where he hides in a cave, deep underground. And it is an amazing thing, sir, it is said that under the Mountains of the Moon in Zaire is this great city of copper, of many thousands of shining buildings. There dwells the god Umbaba or Jabulon. And this god is waiting for the day when the surface of the Earth will be cleared of human beings so that he, and his children, the Chitauli, can come out and enjoy the heat of the Sun. And, one day, sir, I had a very unexpected visit while I was living in Soweto, near Johannesburg. I was visited by priests from Tibet. One of these priests, I'm sure you have met him or you know of him. His name is Akyong Rinpochce. He is one of the leading Tibetan priests in England who was exiled with the Dalai Lama, and he visited me one day while I was in my medicinal village in Soweto. And one of the things that Akyong Rinpochce asked me was, "Do I know of a secret city which is somewhere in Africa, a city made of copper?" I said, "But, Akyong, you are describing the city of Umbaba, the city of the

*unseen god, the god who hides underground. How do you know about this?"
And Akyong Rinpochce... told me that at one time the great Lama left Tibet
with a group of followers and came to Africa searching for this city. And
the Lama, and his followers, were never seen again. They never returned to
Tibet. Now, sir, we have got stories in central and southern Africa about little
Yellow men who came to Africa looking for the city of Umbaba...*

Mutwa says a figure named Jabulon (Jah-Baal-on) leads "the Chitauli".
These Chitauli are identified, by Mutwa, as a race of Reptilian beings.
Mutwa claims that the words Chitauli and Jabulon are words given by
Africans. I was familiar with Jabulon, but had never heard of Chitauli.

An initial search did not bring up the word Chitauli, but again, digging
deeper, I found the "sky god" Chido who, in some cultures, is also linked
to snakes and serpents, sky serpents and rainbow serpents. Mutwa was
presumably saying "Chidoli" and it was transcribed as Chitauli. Moreover,
the word Chid, Chit, Shit, Sit, Set is the ancient word for what we today
call Satan.

At first, I found no indication that the word Jabulon was Africa-made.
But the book on African Mythology helped here too. One of the "gods"
of African lore is called Djaba. Another god is called Bulane and another
Buluku. My guess is that Djaba-Bulane became Ja-Bulon.

Non-African teachings know of a "one-eyed-God", as I've shown in my
book *Levels of Heaven and Hell*. Cross-cultural alignments are for me
indicators whether a person is just making things up or referencing some
kind of ancient truth. It took me a few hours of research, but so far
everything Mutwa said could be verified.

The more you know, the easier it is to cross-reference. Had I written this
book thirty years ago, a time when I was actually interested in Reptilians,
I wouldn't have had enough knowledge to know where to look, but today
finding things out is a walk in the park.

Even so, a thorough search brought up nothing about a copper city below Rwenzori mountains. A part of me wanted to dismiss the story, but my intuition kept tugging at me, telling me to have a *closer* look.

Credo Mutwa says the Chitauli are responsible for oppressing humanity. He says reptilians have spiritual and physical manifestations and in their physical form, they mate with humans. Their offspring hybrids are put into positions of power on Earth. I guess that explains why most political elites are socially awkward and emotionally cold. On social media they struggle to sound human, using corporate jargon, stilted political lingo and manners of communicating that are completely out of touch with normal human beings. The popularity of Donald Trump is partially explained in that he spoke like a normal human being–straightforward, unpretentious and sometimes slightly vulgar, with very little care about crafting a clean public image.

Later in the book, the topic is referenced once more as part of an interview:

I would like to go back to the copper city for a moment. It would seem that this Jabulon would be the equivalent of what, in the West, we call Satan. Would you say that?

Credo Mutwa: *I think so, yes, sir. He is the chief of the Chitauli. And, like Satan, he lives in a house underground where great fires are always lighted, to keep him warm. Because, we are told, that after the great war they fought with God, they became cold in their blood and they cannot stand freezing weather, which is why they require human blood, and also they require fire always to be kept working where they are.*

Mutwa has been sharing on Reptilians long before it became popular in our culture. He was born in 1921 and published his first book in 1964. Someone who was talking about it before it became culturally acceptable deserves some respect.

He doesn't say it, but I take from his description that the copper city was built by one people and then taken over by another. The *Imanyukela* built it and the *Chitauli* now run it.

But again, the question that always drives me is: Is there any evidence? As much as I enjoy far-out stories, it's no fun without tangible proof.

Looking around the area today, I found the Kilembe copper mines at the foot of Rwenzori Mountains. That's good news. If extraterrestrials built a copper city, there must be copper there. And if there is copper, there must also be copper mining. I also learned that the modern Tibetans are interested in the mines! From a 2015 news article:

China's Tibet-Hima Industries Consortium is set to begin copper mining at the Kilembe Mines in Uganda in May 2015.

The Kilembe Mines in southwestern Uganda are rich in copper and cobalt deposits.

The consortium took over operations of the mine from Kilembe Mines Limited in 2013, and since, has been executing technical work on the mines, according to project officials. The Chinese consortium had also committed to invest US$175mn towards the rehabilitation of the mine and upgrade a power plant to assist mine operations.

Source: https://www.africanreview.com/construction-a-mining/quarrying/ chinese-consortium-to-begin-work-on-ugandan-copper-mine

It's rare that things are this straightforward. Ancient Tibetans were interested in Rwenzori, modern Tibetans are still interested!

Three years later, the deal with the Tibetans was cancelled, and they sought $33 Million in damages (1). According to the Ugandan Government, they were running a Gold Smuggling Ring (2). But another article says they were shut down over environmental non-compliance (3). Later court cases show that the Ugandan Royal Family were behind getting rid of the Tibetans, saying the Government never had the right to give away the mines (4). In other news, minerals have been stolen from the mines (5) and mysterious deaths reported there (6).

Sources:

1. https://ugbusiness.com/2018/03/companies/chinese-firm-wants-33m-for-termination-of-kilembe-mines-deal#gref
2. https://observer.ug/business/55966-govt-busts-gold-smuggling-ring-at-kilembe-mines.html
3. https://www.kfm.co.ug/news/kilembe-mines-closed-over-environmental-non-compliance.html
4. https://www.monitor.co.ug/uganda/news/national/court-verdict-casts-shadow-over-kilembe-mines-deal-3343618
5. https://observer.ug/news/headlines/67107-kilembe-mineral-samples-go-missing-minister-calls-for-investigation
6. https://observer.ug/business/38-business/41753-kilembe-mines-stops-work-after-2-deaths

With this many contradictory stories, you know something is amiss. What were the Tibetans really doing there?

A strange side-note regarding the Chitauli: I discovered that the surname Sitoli is the most common in Nepal and the second most common in India. But for some strange reason, it is also used in Uganda.

If we accept Nepal as part of Tibetan culture, this is yet another Tibet-Uganda connection that is difficult to explain.

I've marked the location of the Rwenzori mountains, the "world seat of the Reptilians", if Mutwa is to be believed, with a red circle, right at an oddly named town called "Fort Portal":

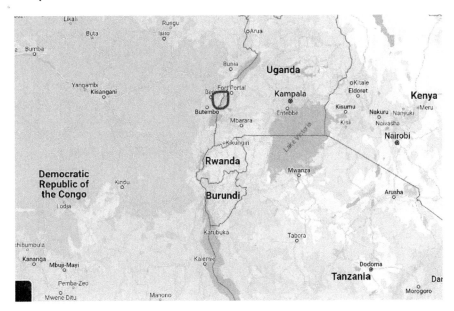

Why do I say Fort Portal is oddly named? Because the royal family of Uganda, who lay claim to the copper mines, are the *Tooro* family. The ancient and modern German word for Portal is *Tor*. Nearby, we also find twin mountains called Portal Peaks. And as if that weren't enough about Portals, a 1966 earthquake in the Rwenzori Mountains was called the *Toro* Earthquake.

We have four references to the mountains being a gate. A gate to where? A dimensional travel portal? A stargate? Rumor has it, the Reptilians don't like to use regular flight but materialize and dematerialize at different locations by using portals.

Royal families of Africa shouldn't be underestimated. Their lineage and documentation of events goes back hundreds of years, sometimes even a thousand. A people who have a recorded awareness of what happened 600, 400 or even 200 years ago, have certain knowledge that awards them advantages over people who don't know what happened before.

Who knows, they may have checked their royal ancient records and found out about the copper city and then chased away the Tibetans.

This is a map of Africa drawn in Basel, Switzerland, in 1550.

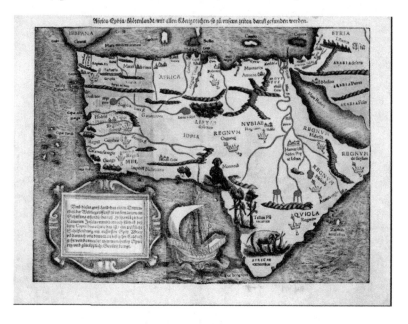

Credo Mutwa claims that this place was the seat of an extraterrestrial race, a place of origin. If that were true, we'd find evidence of it on old maps. A closer look reveals this:

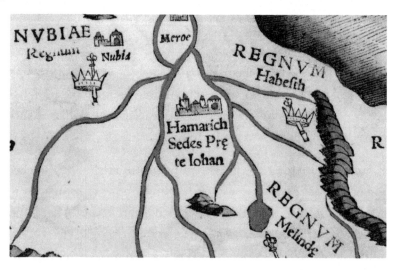

We see that Africa is split into kingdoms (Regnum). At the place which roughly corresponds to where Uganda is today, we see a city titled Hamarich Sedes Prete Iohan. This is Portugese and means the seat (sedes) of the vigilant ruler (hamarich) priest (prete) John (iohan). It's the only place in Africa indicated as some kind of governmental seat.

This is a cut-out from a 1640 map drawn in Amsterdam:

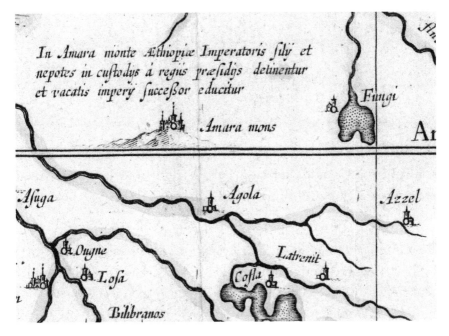

The map shows an Africa of cities and kingdoms, many of which are today forgotten. But some names still exist today, such as the town of Agola, which is above Lake Victoria in today's Uganda. Above it we find the mountain range of Uganda, which is today Rwenzori:

Agola in Uganda on Google Maps:

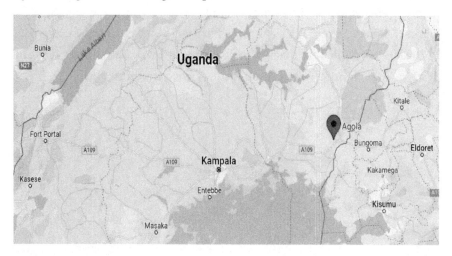

The seat of the Government in the old map is in Uganda. It's in the mountains of Uganda, north of Lake Victoria and it's called Amara mons. The geography of the lakes has changed slightly since then, maybe through cataclysm.

The Latin text roughly says "In Amara is mounted the Emperor of Ethiopia, daughter and grandchildren, custodians of the king president are detained and free. The empire brought out a successor". Amara mons translates as "bitter mountain" or "bitter moon". Ethiopia was the old name for a large part of Africa, not just one country. "Mons" may refer to the moon, as even today, Rwenzori are named "mountains of the moon".

By 1688 Amara mons was still shown on maps but no longer described as the seat of Africa:

By 1720 the seat of Africa had disappeared from maps:

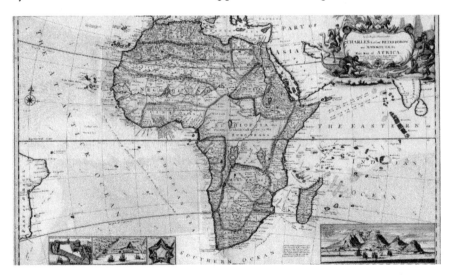

The mapmakers of the 1700s go out of their way to say that the area is "wholly unknown to Europeans":

That's an odd thing to write on a map and also a lie. I've shown how a town known in the 1600s (Agola), a lake known in the 1600s (Victoria) and a mountain range known in the 1600s are still there today. Why would the mapmakers of the 1700s change their story and claim the region is wholly unknown to Europeans? What is so controversial about Central Africa for the Europeans to lie about it?

By 1805 any awareness of the old kingdoms and the former geography had further vanished. From the 1700s onward, knowledge was regressing.

This map doesn't even acknowledge Lake Victoria which is yet to be "discovered".

This, in and of itself, proves the faking of history. It's likely that the known African kingdoms and cities were destroyed in a war, cataclysm or both. Then, as if in a "reset", Africa had to be "discovered" all over again.

Credo Mutwa said the ancient aliens ruled from the Rwenzori mountains. Ancient maps show precisely that spot as the seat of Government over much of Africa. While none of this directly proves Mutwa's stories, the facts do align with them. It's easy to punch holes through the story of liars with just a little research, but so far Mutwas' story holds up.

The most common story of Ugandan Mythology is called *The King of Snakes*. The story is taught across tribes and to schoolchildren. The story is about the King of Snakes living "on the hillside" of Uganda and "coming down" every day to eat people in the village. Its name was Sesota. To defeat the snake, the villagers use a child as bait and manage to entrap the snake in a large pot of water. Then they burnt the great snake. Ancient tales of victory over serpents are found in every culture.

Another popular myth of Uganda is *the story of Kintu*. It's about a king and his family who lived in "cloud land". One daughter of the sky king, Gulu, came down to Earth to marry a human man by the name of Kintu. They'd have lived a happy life if it weren't for Walumbe, another sky king, who didn't like humans and sought to spoil their happiness. Kintu told Walumbe that if he leaves them alone, he will sacrifice his first child to him. Ever since then, Walumbe returns from time to time to abduct a child.

Remarkably, every time there are ancient or modern tales of Reptilians, there are also murmurings of child abduction and child sacrifice. From this we can surmise that human children are their preferred food.

The Royal Family laying claim to the region since 1822 is the Tooro Kingdom. They are a breakaway of the Bunyoro Kingdom which is said to have ruled the area from the 1300s onward. The Bunyoro are successors of the Chwezi Kingdom who are said to have ruled there from the year 500 onward (Wezi is ancient German for knowledge, wizardy, magic). The Chwezi are traditionally viewed as "supernatural beings" or "people from the sky".

As in other cultures, what makes a royal family royal is their claimed descendancy from extraterrestrials. Not all modern royals are consciously aware of this, but I know some that are.

It's said the Tutsi people of Rwanda and Burundi (directly neighboring the Rwenzori mountains), who were mass-murdered in the Rwandan genocides, thought themselves descendants of these sky-people. It's claimed the Tutsi preferred a caste-system of society, in which they were at the top and the Hutu at the bottom, based on their relation to the sky-gods. Other Tutsi deny this, calling it propaganda to stoke tensions between the two tribes. Some deny there is any difference between the tribes at all. Whatever the truth, the countries around Rwenzori mountains are by far the most troubled in the world. Congo has been called the poorest nation in the world by economists. It has among the highest violent crime rate. But if it truly were the seat of the "Reptilian Overlords", I guess that's to be expected. The most troubled areas of the Democratic Republic of Congo are in fact Eastern Congo precisely around the Rwenzori mountains. Tourism in Congo is rare, but if tourists venture there, they are warned to stick to the western part of the country, avoiding the East. There we find "blood diamond" activity, child soldiers, child diamond mining and other evils as sponsored by non-African mining companies (despite false claims of the Government of DR Congo that child labor is not permitted).

In Africa and elsewhere, the ancient earthly rulers required approval from above, from higher beings, sky people or "the heavens". The kings and rulers of old, if the chronologies are to be believed, were first "gods", then "demi gods" (the offspring of marriages between people from the sky and people on Earth). Some Africans still think this way. They don't believe in modern politics and Government. To them, the royal class are the real rulers and politicians are only figureheads. In "western culture" it's the other way around: We think that royals are only figureheads whereas the real power lies with the politicians.

Quoting from Wikipedia on the Chwezi Kingdom:

According to oral traditions of western Uganda, the Kitara empire naturally known as the Empire of the Sun, Empire of the Moon disintegrated during the 14th-15th centuries, and broke up into new autonomous kingdoms ruled by descendants of the Chwezi who, by oral legend, mysteriously vanished without a trace. The new kingdoms included Bunyoro, Tooro, Ankole, Buganda, Busoga in Uganda, the Kingdom of Rwanda, Burundi, and Karagwe in northern Tanzania and others in the eastern Democratic Republic of Congo. Kitara was reported to have been ruled by two dynasties, the Batembuzi gods and their successors the Bachwezi god-kings. The Chwezi dynasty is thought to have been related to a Tembuzi king Ngonzaki's son Isaza. Isaza is believed to have been the last ruler of the Batembuzi dynasty, he married Nyamata, the daughter of Nyamiyonga, "King of the underworld". This union produced king Isimbwa who later fathered Ndahura in Runyakitara (known in Rwanda as Ndahiro I Bamara and in Buganda as Wamala Ndawula), the first of the Chwezi dynastic kings. King Ngonzaki was son to King Bada. Bada was the son to Kakama (Kayima) whose father Hanga descended from the heavens.

The Chwezi "mysteriously vanished without a trace". This aligns with Mutwa's assertion that the extraterrestrials abruptly left, to return to their star constellation. Later, the kingdom was infiltrated through intermarriage by the "king of the underworld", which Mutwa calls the Boss of the Chitauli (Reptilians), Jabulon and Ugandan Mythology calls "King of Snakes" and "Walumbe". In addition, old maps confirm the Kingdom as a seat of a much larger area and the subsequent disappearance and cover-up.

While researching this chapter I found a website called "rwenzori international hotels". I won't print a link to it here because it seems rather suspicious to me. The title of the page:

EXPERIENCE LUXURY AT THE RWENZORI INTERNATIONAL HOTEL SILVER CITY, UNITED STATES

Further below, we read:

Book Rwenzori International Hotel for a Relaxing Getaway in Uganda.

The **Rwenzori International Hotel Silver City United States** is an elegant hotel located in the heart of downtown Silver City. This luxurious 4-star establishment offers a modern and stylish design, with a touch of traditional charm. The accommodations feature spacious rooms and suites, each appointed with all the amenities one would expect from a high-end hotel. Guests can enjoy complimentary Wi-Fi and cable television throughout their stay, while also taking advantage of the onsite fitness center or relaxing in the outdoor heated pool. Additionally, guests have access to three restaurants that serve up delectable international cuisine as well as several bars for evening libations. The Rwenzori International Hotel truly provides its visitors with everything they need for an unforgettable stay in Silver City!

The address is in Silver City, New Mexico:

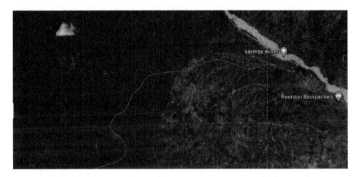

But the link that says "Book Now" actually goes to a booking.com page for a hotel in Kasese, Uganda, which is adjacent to the Kilembe Copper mines.

The page makes no sense at all. Is the Hotel in Silver City, New Mexico, as the website says? I checked and found no such hotel in New Mexico.

Credo Mutwa said that the copper city is surrounded by a silver wall. One might also call it Silver City.

Is the webpage some kind of coded message to people who wish to visit the ancient subterranean city near Kasese, Uganda? Or is it just a misguided attempt at search-engine-optimization?

A Google Maps view of the small copper mining town Kilembe reveals roads that start as normal ones in Kilembe but are then shown continuing where there are no roads on the surface. This is a Google error or an indication of subterranean roads.

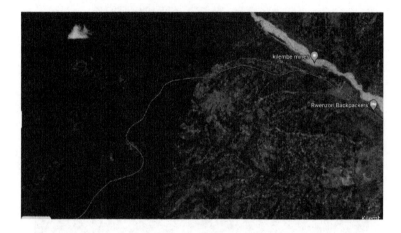

Today Ruwenzori Mountains have little meaning to anyone outside of trekking and wildlife watching, but in old books we find that our ancestors ascribed a deeper meaning to the area.

According to Persian mythology, the Peri is a winged creature, higher in rank than demons (jinn) but not high enough to gain entrance to Heaven until they have done penance or atoned for their sins. The Irish poet Thomas Moore (born 1779) once wrote a poem of one Peri who tried to gain entry to heaven by "stealing the sigh" of a maiden who had died of the plague in the Ruwenzori mountains. Why would a virgin who died in Ruwenzori impress the gatekeepers of Heaven? Is it because this is where "those who came from the sky" built their first seat of Government?

In 1849 Henry David Thoreau compared the Mountains of the Moon, the Rocky Mountains, and the Himalayas (which he spelled

"Himmaleh", ancient German word for Heaven) as having "a kind of personal importance in the annals of the world". But why?

There is an 1849 Poem *Eldorado* by Edgar Allan Poe. Eldorado is a lost ancient city of gold and the subject of countless legends. It was supposed to have been hidden somewhere in South America. But the poem tells us otherwise:

Gaily bedight,
A gallant knight,
In sunshine and in shadow,
Had journeyed long,
Singing a song,
In search of Eldorado.

But he grew old — This knight so bold —
And o'er his heart a shadow —
Fell as he found
No spot of ground
That looked like Eldorado.

And, as his strength,
Failed him at length,
He met a pilgrim shadow —
'Shadow,' said he,
* Where can it be—*
This land of Eldorado?'

'Over the Mountains
Of the Moon,
Down the Valley of the Shadow,
Ride, boldly ride,'
The shade replied, — 'If you seek for Eldorado!'

Edgar Allan Poe says that this lost and legendary land of precious metals can be found "over the mountains of the moon".

According to a Survey paper titled *Management of Sacred Sites in Rwenzori Mountains* the traditional beliefs of the people living in the region include a Taboo on "taking a radio into the mountains", "having sexual intercourse in the mountains", "crossing the mountain from one end to another in one day", "looking from side to side while moving through the mountains" and "leaving fire burning after a ritual sacrifice". Such peculiar taboos, nearly incomprehensible to outsiders. Each of these taboos are linked to "energy", be it the energy of radio-waves, sexuality, attention or the intense emotion emanated by the creature being sacrificed.

Alas, I did not find the subterranean copper city, nor evidence of reptilian activity. I'd have also loved to explore the mountains with Google Earth, but relevant places are cloud-covered or blacked-out. One example:

To understand why Tibetans may have been interested in the copper city, I refer readers to an article on my website www.falsehistory.net titled "Ancient maps show the terrestrial paradise". There, I identified Tibet as a probable seat of the ancient "terrestrial paradise", the literal and real Garden of Eden or Shamballa, Shangri-La and other names it has been given. The copper city is perhaps the counterpart to Paradise, the "seat of Satan". I'm just speculating here.

My verdict on Credo Mutwa is that everything he said can be verified by other sources. That doesn't prove reptilian extraterrestrials, but it does encourage further research.

Image: Nuwa and Fuxi, the serpent "Gods" of ancient China.

3

John Of God, Oprah And The Reptilians

In the year 2009 I read a book titled "The Body Snatchers" by someone who calls herself "Susan Reed". The book was amateurishly written and I couldn't find evidence for any of the wild claims it made. I concluded the author was mentally disturbed, even possessed by the very entities she was claiming to expose.

I dismissed the book at the time. Until 2018, when something mentioned in the book became international news. A "miracle healer" and celebrity from Brazil, who called himself "John of God" got arrested. He was widely beloved by the "new age" community, befriended by Oprah Winfrey, Marina Abramovic, Deepak Chopra and many other famous people. Following his arrest, it was learned he was baby-farming (getting women pregnant and selling their babies to the rich), human trafficking, sex trafficking, abusing children sexually, fraud and many other crimes so evil it beggars belief.

The Sun ✓
@TheSun

'John of God' cult leader with millions of followers 'ran sex slave farm and sold babies to highest bidder'

thesun.co.uk/news/8318483/j...

Oprah gave him fame.

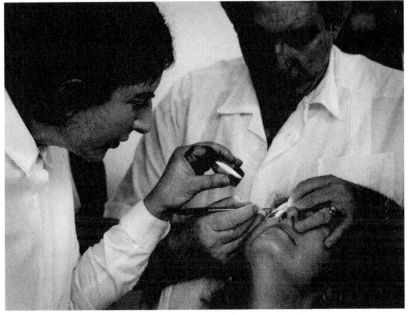

Image: *Abramovic with medium João de Deus (John of God) during an eye psychic surgery in his spiritual healing center.*

At the time Susan Reed published her book on Reptilians in 2009, nobody knew of the evils of "John of God" or Abramovic. Abramovic became well known in the 2015 "pizzagate" affair, where her connection to Oprah Winfrey, Hillary Clinton, Harvey Weinstein, Jeffrey Epstein and John Podesta became known through Wikileaks. Pizzagate revolved around a pedophile-ring, sex-slave trafficking, cannibalism and satanism of the Hollywood-and Washington D.C. Elite. Abramovic, as the world will one day learn is the biological mother of Lady Gaga and cousin of arrested child sex trafficker Ghislaine Maxwell. Or maybe the world won't find out, it doesn't matter to me either way. Nor may the world ever know of the close relation between Ghislaine Maxwell and Anthony Fauci, architect of the 2020-2022 "Covid" hoax. An honest examination of all the people involved would overextend the scope of this book but if you ever decide to do so, you'll find that it's a fairly small club.

In 2009, John of God was revered and beloved across the spectrum of new-age publications. Understandably, in this environment, Susan Reed's book was a flop. Nobody wanted to hear that this miracle healer was a psychopathic criminal. Upon hearing the news, I purchased the book again. No matter how poorly the book was written, an author that can make those kinds of predictions at a time nobody believed them was onto something!

I quote directly from Susan Reed's book (Ettish and Mary Magdalene are the names of various reptilian entities):

John of God healing and psychic surgery centre in Brazil.

I went on a two week healing tour to this centre. Ettissh, at this point, was being held in the spirit realm. Obviously, he was in hiding from the organisation. Rather than healing me, an entity from the centre attached to me on my way home. This entity's name was Mary Magdalene and was the overseeing entity of the centre. She had a powerful presence and believed I had discovered a secret of theirs. Disgracefully rather than healing me Mary Magdalene was enticed by the reptilian to work for him. He would give away reptilian secrets and information to her in exchange. They made plans together to get Brian in trouble, with lies that would blame Brian for what the reptilian entity had caused, she at the same time as working for him, was working against the reptilian organisation and caused this book. Lies were going to be told. The reptilian entity had caused the secret about karma to be discovered by the spirit realm, but they were going to blame Brian. The reptilian entity gave away other secrets to Mary to entice her to work for him. She worked against me, harassing me greatly, whilst all the time she herself worked against the reptilians.

Increasing world belief in spirits.

John of God the psychic surgeon and healer, is advertised worldwide. Many mediums advertise healing tours there in numerous magazines such as Psychic news, kindred Spirit, Caduceus. There are tours advertised on the internet and I attended a video and lecture whilst in California. They encourage everyone throughout the world to go there and promise healing of all and every condition. I remember when I first heard of John of God at the lecture in California, I was impressed by the video of the psychic surgery with John of God using a knife in someone's eye without anesthetic. What I questioned was their prescription of herbs for healing: all the herbs are identical was what the lecturer said and everyone gets given them and they heal every individual condition. The lecturer made a joke about this obviously herself finding identical herbs a bit strange. They are blessed by the entity, the entity being the spirit who works through John of God. Why not give different herbs for different conditions I thought like Chinese medicine. Overall, I was impressed by the video and lecturer and made a decision to go for my own healing. My healing need was the complete disconnection of the reptilian entity. I was encouraged again and again to go but the financial cost of it was off-putting. The tours that they recommended for first timers were 1300 dollars and then there was the flight on top costing 600 pounds. I work as a healthcare worker in hospitals where the wages are not high. Where I was visiting in California, people had to save up for some time to go, it was a community where the wages were low. So, because I couldn't afford to go I didn't for a year. When my finances improved I contacted Robert Pellegrino who advertises on the internet and had written the book" The Miracle man of Brazil" about John of God. Having written a book, I trusted that he would be the best person to go on a tour with. I told him my problem, and he assured me that it would be healed and encouraged me to go. So, I saved up and went on his two-week tour with great hope. There were about 20 people in my tour with a wide range of illnesses or just life problems as I said everyone is encouraged to go with any condition. Some of my group was in financial hardship and it upset me the lengths they had to go to, to get the money. One man was a DJ and had had to sell all his musical equipment to go, another man was unemployed due to his illness and had to borrow the money. Several visits were also recommended which runs into thousands of pounds. The second day we were taken to see the "entity". We queued up in a very long queue. I felt sick with nerves as I approached John of God; I was surprised at my feelings as I would have expected to feel good seeing a healer. There was something about the entity that scared me. I had about 5 seconds in front of the entity who didn't even look at me and I was told to sit in the meditation room. I sat there waiting for my healing but nothing happened. I left the "casa" as it is called very disappointed. I wasn't the only one in the group disappointed; another lady was in tears feeling that she had been given no healing at all. John of God is just one man, and he is the only healer and sees hundreds of patients a day! Two thirds of the patients are local Brazilians, the poor who see John of god as we would see a doctor. These were the people who were given more time in front of the entity, he would hold their hand and talk with them. A few minutes was spent where as the "foreigners" were whisked by in a few seconds. I experienced this again when trying to see John of God the man, I waited outside his office and despite being first in the queue, and the local Brazilians were given preference. I suppose this is understandable, the healing is for the poor Brazilians and there is only so much healing one man can do. But then foreigners should not be encouraged to go. So why are they encouraged to go in masses? This is for a reason that is the hidden agenda of John of God healing. Their agenda is not just healing; it is increasing world belief in spirits. So, foreigners are encouraged there for the purpose of making them believe in spirits, the healing of foreigners is not the objective although undoubtedly some are healed...

So, I continue. Having been in front of the entity once and without being healed I became very upset. I experienced uncontrollable crying in the meditation rooms, feeling very disappointed. This was obviously unacceptable. I was meant to be being healed and certainly bad P. R for the Casa. So, the second time I went in front of the entity I was told to sit in the room next to the entity where intense healing and psychic surgery took place. I was very pleased to at last be getting healing. But I was given no healing and instead a pretense of healing was put on just to stop me crying. After this session still not healed I confronted the Casa that they had pretended my healing. This went down like a "ton of bricks" and I was subjected to near instant psychic attack." We are too busy" I was told as an explanation and it seemed very similar to the National Health Service Hospital I had been working in - too many patients and not enough time. Thereafter I was made to feel very unwelcome, I still had a week of the tour left and had no choice but to stay. The Casa obviously had methods to deter unwanted people from staying, a self-defense method that made the unwelcome guest extremely uncomfortable. I became guarded by spirits who appeared red and unpleasant. At one time I was taking a walk by myself and an entity attacked my heart/lung area. The John of God Casa is subjected to a lot of attack from Lawyers, police and has managed to keep going despite this. This self-defense strategy must be part of the reason and I will explain later the extent that the self-defense goes to and is shocking.

An observation that I made that I thought rather odd was the treatment of relatives of the sick. Some of the very sick came along with a relative. These relatives were in fact not sick and yet were all prescribed herbs. Why were they prescribed herbs? They had no illness to cure. No explanation was given. One lady in our group who was caring for her paralyzed son met me in tears after going in front of the entity who had asked her was she taking the herbs. She had in fact been given no herbs and the entity red faced had to suddenly switch her on to herbs. Her faith in the healing power of the herbs had been shattered and also the healing of her son. It seemed to me that healthy relatives were being given herbs not for the purpose of healing. So, do the herbs heal? At that point I wasn't much interested.

John of God in league with the reptilian Ettissh : Ettissh recruits help/ a book gets written.

On completion of the tour, I left for home extremely disappointed. John of God had identified a long-distance connection with a reptilian but had not removed it. As I was leaving the Casa an entity from the Casa followed me home. It had replaced my spirit guide who was taken from me at the Casa and who I have never seen since! They say the healing continues for several weeks after the visit and I was hopeful that perhaps the reptilian would now be disconnected. This was not the purpose of the entities presence. I later discovered from Archangel Uriel via his channel Jennifer Hoffman that the entities name was Mary Magdalene and that she oversees John of God. She is a big and powerful spirit and had dark motives for attaching to me. She believed I had discovered one of the secrets of the Casa which is the herbs are just placebo, in other words have no healing power and are used because people expect medicine. Ettissh was also threatening to have the reptilians publicize in newspapers about these herbs. She greatly feared newspaper articles believing that it would damage John of God.

She was certainly neurotic and had weaknesses and I became subjected to a shocking attack and harassment lasting a year. She teamed up with the reptilian performing psychic surgery on me to place the reptilian Ettissh into my aura and body. I had gone to John of God with a long-distance weak connection to Ettissh and the result of the trip was to now have a far worse entity attached to me and a reptilian in my aura. David Ashworth in "Dancing with the Devil" says that once you have one it is the thin edge of the wedge and it attracts more and this is certainly what happened to me at John of God and I think my story needs to be told. I have evidence of her presence as I said Archangel Uriel identified her, the Spiritualist Church had a psychic artist draw her, the head of a leading spirit release organization identified her as satanic and from John of God.

How the entity from the John of God healing treated me is absolutely diabolical, I went there for healing and to join forces with a reptilian to harm me is disgraceful. The entity from there was far more powerful than the reptilian so the John of God psychic surgery centre wrecked my life for a year.

Ettissh would also give away reptilian secrets and information to her in exchange. They made plans together to get Brian in trouble, with lies that would blame Brian for what the reptilian entity had caused. Other lies were going to be told. The reptilian entity had caused the secret about karma to be discovered by the spirit realm but they were going to blame Brian. The reptilian entity gave away other secrets to Mary to entice her to work for him. She at the same time as working for him was working against the reptilian organisation and caused this book.

She wanted this book published, and she went to great lengths to have it published, she edited it and pushed it to completion, even writing against them herself. This book was completed at her hands. Showing off to Mary and stuck in his reptilian problem of "have to win over me" Ettissh cares nothing for the reptilian organisation and is an absolute liability; having to hide from them for three years I suppose says it all...

I returned to John of God after a year and confronted Robert Pellegrino about the entity attaching from John of God. He admitted it does happen and had even happened to him for two weeks!, but didn't offer a solution..

I have a Will with everything in and this book will be increased in circulation if I need to use my Will however the cause of my death will have been the John of God psychic surgery centre. And I must make it very clear that I would never in a million years commit suicide, I don't believe in it. I am also in very good health and am young.

I now see the works of this author in a different light. Rather than a delusional nutjob, I see a simple and well-intended person who had come under entity-influence, reporting her direct experience. Her account is authentic and proven by what emerged about John of God ten years later. She had been a lone voice warning about him. The type of people connected to John of God are an indication that Reptilians could be real and this author knew about them.

I view the direct experiences of "regular folk", even simple-minded folk, as more trustworthy than the works of many superstar-authors. Simple people are usually not involved in psyops, propaganda, misdirection, hype or manipulation. Their direct-experience reports are invaluable.

Susan Reed was a pen name. Her real name was Jennifer Gosbell, and she was a hairdresser from England who "died under mysterious circumstances". The only photo I found of this unknown hero:

I found only one local news article about her death. The article was posted to the "Birmingham Live" website on March 29, 2010, one year after she published the book:

Was alien obsessed Midland woman murdered in Bahamas?

A Midland dietician who claimed she was possessed by aliens has died mysteriously in the Bahamas—sparking fears she may have been murdered.

Jennie Gosbell's lifeless body was discovered floating in the calm sea off Cable Beach at Guanahani Village, Nassau.

Police believed the 44-year-old, from Birmingham, drowned while out swimming shortly before being found by a jet ski operator. And they have ruled out homicide.

But her mum Susan Gosbell, from Hemel Hempstead, has told the Sunday Mercury that she believes that the reasons her daughter died are far more sinister. And she says that tourism chiefs on the paradise isle have "brushed this under the carpet" to protect the idyllic image they present to the world.

Susan said that it doesn't make sense that Jennie died by drowning because she was a strong swimmer. And, even more suspicious, her passport, bag, money and personal belongings had all gone missing.

Susan, who has two other children, said she wants thorough investigation into whether someone attacked her daughter. And she is especially concerned due to a book her daughter wrote in which she claims she is exposing aliens' plans to take over the world.

Susan said Jennie believed she had been taken over by 'reptilian aliens' and learned of their sinister scheme during this experience. She wrote the book called The Body snatchers using her mum's maiden name, Susan Reed. And Susan's spooky X Files type claims are supported by a wide circle of Jennie's friends. Susan, who had to fly to Nassau to identify her daughter's body, said: "Jennie was a fit girl and a strong swimmer, so I find it hard to believe that she just drowned.

"She had just been to a cashpoint and drawn out 200 dollars before going for a swim, yet all her money, passport, make-up, shoes and even the birthday card she always carried with her had disappeared.

"There was nothing left in her bag or hotel room to show who she was. I tried to talk to the police in the Bahamas, but they didn't want to know and obviously didn't like having a dead body that might affect tourism.

"They tried to give an impression that she was acting a little strangely and blundering along, but she was taking some time out after writing a sci-fi book and was planning another.

"She had gone out there for a yoga resort and was then travelling around and planning to go to Florida.

"After she died, a cheque came from the sales of her book in the post, it was very sad.

"It is awful not knowing what really happened to her.

Jennie worked as a dietician for Birmingham Nutrition and Dietetics Service, and treated patients at Moseley Hall Hospital and across north and east of the city.

But she was due to face a disciplinary hearing in front of the Health Profession's Council (HPC) when she took a break to the Bahamas on her own.

She was found dead on the morning of October 8 last year.

The HPC has now cancelled the hearing, which was for a catalogue of failings dating back to 2007 and 2008 in Birmingham.

Allegations against Jennie included wrongly advising a patient to drink a whole bottle of medicine, not reviewing the feed she had prescribed, wrongly concluding a patient with a superbug was vomiting due to chemotherapy, using the work photocopier for personal use and poor record-keeping.

Jennie had stayed at various places in New Providence, in the Bahamas before finally staying at the Blue Water Resort, in Cable Beach, where her body was found in the surrounding waters after going for a swim.

Friends have claimed that after writing Body Snatchers: A True Story of Body Snatching by the Reptilians—A Real Alien Conspiracy, Jennie complained that she had been warned that she would be 'removed'.

The book described her experiences with "Reptilian entities and their human-hybrid lackeys" who use weapons to target people, and they say victims include a famous actress who had recently died but was rumored to have committed suicide.

Reptilians are believed to have begun to evolve on Earth millions of years ago from small dinosaurs.

Ellis C Taylor, an author on the paranormal who runs his own website, Looking Into The Dark Places, said: "Jennie was tracked by aliens, like something seen on the X Files.

"She died in very strange circumstances and it is very bizarre.

"Considering what she wrote, it makes the death even odder and I suspect there's been a cover up.

"Jennie had integrity and was very caring and she felt comfortable talking to me about the encounters she had without any judgement.

"It saddened me to hear about her death."

Another fan of Jennie's work wrote a tribute stating: "She is one of the most respected and honourable authors and gifted writers on this planet, and is known worldwide for her collaboration with the reptilian resistance movement.

"Her death has been linked to reptilian activity because she exposed their plans in detailed terms in her book The Body Snatchers.

"After the reptilians lost their battle in the war against humanity, they realized that they couldn't deny that they had lost so now they're after those researchers who aren't part in one way or another of their agenda or who are not related to them by any means.

"Susan only wrote the book because she felt that her life was threatened and by publishing the book, she would provide herself a modicum of protection."

Jennie's book, which she said was based on her own life, told the story of Susan Reed who became romantically involved with a man called Brian.

In the book Brian is a reptilian host who assigned two interdimensional reptilians to spy on Susan and report her activities back to Brian.

He later tells her, he was a perfectly normal human until an abduction where he was taken in a light beam up into an alien spacecraft and replaced.

Neil Hague, a book illustrator who designed the cover of Jennie's novel, said: "It is terrible to hear of the death.

"Jennie had a lot of fears and anxieties and sent an email to me and some other people appealing for help in 2008 because she felt like she was being followed and under some pressure. She felt like she was struggling with things."

Jennie's family have been working with the Foreign Office to get reports from the Bahamas on the death for Herfordshire Coroner's Court.

An inquest into the death takes place on Wednesday.

Source: https://www.birminghammail.co.uk/news/local-news/was-alien-obsessed-midland-woman-murdered-246643

A more focused read of her book, revealed to me claims so specific they were worth investigating. *Specifics* is something lacking in "new age" literature, because specifics can either be proven or debunked. I'll list some of her claims below and add commentary to each.

"In ancient days reptilians were more physically present, including as winged dragons".

This claim is probably true. From a medieval Dictionary:

dragon 3

drag'on (drăg'ŭn), n. [OF., fr. L. *draco*, *-onis*, fr. Gr. *drakōn*.] **1.** *Now Rare.* A huge serpent. **2.** A fabulous animal, generally a monstrous winged scaly serpent, lizard, or saurian. **3.** A fierce or very strict person, esp. a woman; a duenna. **4.** Any of several plants of the arum family popularly associated with dragons. **5.** A word used in the Authorized Version to translate several Hebrew forms, some of which are translated by *jackal* or *serpent* in the Revised Version. **6.** Formerly, a short musket carried hooked to a soldier's belt; also, a soldier carrying such a musket. **7.** An armored tractor. **8.** Any of a genus (*Draco*) of small arboreal lizards of the East Indies and southern Asia. Some of the hind ribs, on each side, are prolonged and covered with weblike skin, aiding them in leaping from tree to tree; — called also *flying dragon*. **9.** [cap.] *Astron.* The constellation Draco.

Dragon, as represented in Heraldry.

"Reptilians are working with NASA to create a force field in space to entrap souls so that they can't ascend."

I don't have the resources to either prove or disprove this one. There are things in Jennifers books that seem like fear-mongering from her entities, not genuine knowledge. It is my view, based on plenty of research that, at mid to high consciousness-levels, a soul can't be entrapped and even at low levels it's very difficult to do so.

"The Reptilian agenda is to turn many humans into better slaves. One of their means to do so is through replacing breastfeeding with formula. Baby formula is one of their many tools to dumb down the populace. Baby formula lacks EFAs (essential fatty acids)".

This rang true to me. I researched it a little and found that it's supported by scientific studies. One example:

Methods: This study involved 111 healthy girls, aged 7 to 9 years, who were recruited from nine government and private schools in Dammam, Kingdom of Saudi Arabia. Raven's Coloured Progressive Matrices were used to measure the participants' IQs, and the Vineland Social Maturity Assessment was used to measure their SI through individual interviews. Anthropometric measurements were obtained using standard methods.

Results: The breastfed group showed a greater number of above-average IQ test scores (35 vs. 23%; $P = 0.479$) and better SI scores (78 vs. 55%; $P = 0.066$) compared with the bottle-fed group. The number of girls with normal BMIs was significantly higher in the breastfed group than in the bottle-fed (68 vs. 41%; $P = 0.045$) or mixed-fed groups.

Conclusion: Exclusively breastfed girls had higher IQ and SI results compared with bottle-fed girls. However, unlike the BMI differences, these results were not

At some times, throughout researching this book, I laugh out loud at how ultra-paranoid all of this must sound to a "normal" consciousness. But unfortunately, many of the most outlandish claims can be backed up by studies. Why would we mass-feed our children something that dumbs them down? It doesn't make any sense to me. Why are so few people questioning what is being fed to us physically and spiritually? Why would a company offer dumbing-down formula? Why would many Universities avoid doing similar studies? Isn't the baby-formula topic of utmost importance, compared to millions of less important subjects we give our attention to? And why did I receive such incredibly dense and ignorant comments when I posted about this online? One comment said "Some women can't breastfeed. To tell them baby-formula isn't good is misogynist". When I receive comments like this, I wonder if they're made by bots. It's hard for me to fathom that people can be this dumb. But then I click on the person's profile and realize they are probably real people. How is wanting babies—both male and female—to be smart and healthy, "misogynist"? The implication here is also that there are no alternatives to women who don't breastfeed, as if baby-formula were the only option.

But there are plenty of milks more natural than formula. There is animal milk, that the reptilian propagandists claim is "unhealthy" for children, causing "neurological damage". One can also obtain breast milk from "milk banks". And meanwhile there are also more organic baby-formulas, made by people who were aware of the IQ-studies.

"Reptilians promote wheat-based products because there is something in wheat that hardens the arteries."

It is certainly true that reducing wheat (carbs) increases health. This is attested by millions of people who have gone on "keto" and "carnivore" diets for health or beauty reasons. I have personally witnessed meat-based diets heal sickness, overweight, skin-problems, stomach-issues, brain-fog, attention-deficit, fatigue, etc.

"Reptilians cause our soil to lack trace elements."

I could neither prove nor disprove this but leave it here for further research. What I have certainly seen in the fifty years of my life is a trend toward the dumbing down of general intelligence and the degrading of health.

"Rice is very healthy for humans."

As I don't eat much rice, I can neither confirm nor deny. But it can't be denied that the people with the highest life expectancy in the world—the Japanese—are also among the most avid rice eaters.

"Reptilians are all bankers and they keep you in debt because debt draws money away from you. Debt attracts more debt."

I have no doubt that debt attracts more debt. I've also experienced first-hand the trend toward rewarding debt rather than success. Because I have never taken up credit, my entire life (never been in debt), I have no credit score. For this reason, I am banned from car rental in my country (which requires a credit card and credit score), banned from paying traffic tickets online (also requiring a credit card along with a credit score) and many other things. I could write an entire book about how successful and prosperous people such as myself are discriminated against, but I won't do that because too much victim-posturing only serves the reptilian-agenda. Even suggesting that the rich are discriminated against, causes the brainwashed public to laugh and jeer. "Ha! What an entitled moron! The rich are the oppressor, not the oppressed!".

"Reptilians kill scientists and journalists that snoop around."

Yes, scientists and journalists involved in certain topics around human potential or governmental corruption tend to disappear or "get suicided". As a lifelong researcher it has been common for me to discover abandoned websites and social media accounts of conspiracists and ufologists. Surely some of these lost interest in maintaining their website, but most of them don't even contain a "goodbye" note or "we are discontinuing this Blogspot". I've seen not hundreds but thousands of abruptly abandoned research projects along with online obituaries of the deceased person. Arizona Wilder and Susan Reed are but two examples of hundreds I've personally seen.

"People are remote-killed. Reptilians pose as Freemasons so that they can meetup as groups and perform rituals in which they "zap" (remote kill) people. They meet in places such as Royal Albert Hall, London".

There is no doubt that there is a psychopathic element in society that likes to pose as Freemason, Christian, Muslim, Jew and other groups so that they can gather in various halls, temples, churches and buildings without arousing public suspicion. In fact, one of the first considerations of an evil-doer is in the art of disguise. They'll seek out an organization that is either secretive, such as Freemasons, or seen in a positive light, such as Churches, to conduct their "Business".

Again, none of this is meant to insinuate there are reptilians around every corner. It's important to stress that the majority of people are good. Evil is in the absolute minority and gain their power only through the naïve ignorance of the people.

"Reptilians know how to separate the bioplasmic body from the physical body, to place an alien entity life-force matrix within a human body after removing the soul life-force matrix of the human. An alien can hijack the body, be in the driver's seat but the soul is still required for the body to work."

This is a complicated way of describing entity-possession, which I go into in my book "Clearing Entities".

It begs the question what the relation is between lower-astral entities and reptilians. Are they one and the same? Are they a lower rank than reptilians? Are there many forms and creatures, reptilians being only one of them? From my own out-of-body travels and research, here's what I believe: There are many types of disembodied entities, reptilian is one of them. Reptilian however, is the dominating species among the lower-realm Kingdom. Other entities have been used as minions of the overlords.

If all of this sounds like utter madness to you, I understand the sentiment. The majority of people do not perceive any of what I'm writing about here, so to them it must sound like the rantings of an insane person. I appreciate the sentiment and I'm fully aware of how this sounds. But it's also important to understand that, just because you do not perceive something, because it's outside of your frequency-range, just because your "antennas" don't pick up on it, doesn't mean it's not real. In fact, there are many very real things you experience—microwaves, radio, electricity, music, love—that cannot be seen. To say these are not real because you can't see or touch them, is a great limitation.

"Reptilians sometimes collect DNA samples during their sexual encounters with humans."

I have personally experienced the DNA-collecting agenda, as shared in my book "The Pleiades and our Secret Destiny".

"Reptilians hate humans."

Not surprising. The Bible teaches that Lucifer (also called the Dragon and the Serpent) and his fallen angels were envious of human beings. It was originally he who was supposed to inherit the Earth, then it was given to humans.

"Rubber protects against their attacks and renders humans invisible to them,"

Jennifer describes an episode where she made a rubber cloak out of a bathmat, while she was under Reptilian attack. She could then escape her apartment undetected. I'd never heard of this and gave it some thought.

Rubber is used as an insulator that limits the transfer of electricity. Entities are electricity ("smokeless fire" according to the Quran).

The padded cells in mental asylums are often covered by rubber. This could ward off entity-oppression, which appears to be the cause of some mental illnesses.

"Flying long distance can fix your emotional body back up. Flying means you leave part of your emotional body behind and when it catches up, it can rectify itself."

A strange and fascinating claim. I've done many international flights and know from experience how renewing travel can feel. I've experienced it as a "reset" in many cases.

"We create viruses and make them more virile. We want you to think Earth is a bad place."

By now the term "gain of function research" is common.

If true, this shows that the world is really a good place, otherwise reptilians wouldn't want to convince us otherwise.

In spite of the reptilian oppression, I do believe Earth is a positive place and that nature, water, sunlight and human beings are life-giving. I'd be wary of any propaganda that suggests Earth is a prison or an evil place in general. I realize that this book itself and its title might lend credence to the idea that Earth is a dark and evil place. But we must view the reptilian agenda—if it in fact exists—as a mere reaction and rebellion to the positive, life-giving plan of our Creator. I suspect we were put here to help put an end to the reptilian agenda and make this place what it was originally meant to be: Paradise. It is from this viewpoint that I explore Reptilians, not from the viewpoint of denigrating our realm.

"Evil can exist in a high vibrational way. The Reptilians energy can feel high, even though it is evil. They feel high because they come from Heaven. They are in fact Satan from the Bible."

It was very touching to me to read this. I've never explained this to anyone because it's hard to reconcile with linear thought. It's the first time I'd seen anyone address the concept.

As strange as it sounds, I've also experienced an "evil presence" that was at the same time "vibrationally high". It sounds like a paradox because normally evil is low vibration, coming from the dense astral realms. It's as if certain Reptilians still have a piece of Heaven in their aura. From this we understand why there are people on Earth who *worship* the Reptilians. They say "well, evil or not, I've never felt as empowered as in their presence". But there is a force even better, and it's that of the Creator.

For a reason unknown to me, I can intuitively sense the presence of "higher vibe evil". I know when I'm driving past a building with such "people" in it. I can easily tell products, companies and ideologies made by them. I know them when I see them on video. Human beings who are evil are low consciousness, low vibe, without exception. The "high vibe" evil ones are those who are partially of "heavenly offspring", perhaps reptilian. The high-energy gives them an advantage over us mere mortals.

"Reptilians oppress and divert spiritual organizations."

Indeed, every positive movement is subject to diversion. It mostly happens when the original founder of the movement has passed away, when the original spark is no longer there.

"Reptilians cause racial division,"

Most obvious. Categorizing people into different camps with radically different views is a "reptilian thing", not a human one. Human beings seek harmony and compatibility. The greatest fear of the enemy is that people come together, compare notes and unite.

I once talked to a New York Literary agent who was set to have one of my books published at a very large publishing house. I would have become famous overnight. But her terms were unacceptable for any free human. *"You're going to have to decide which genre you are. Right now, you're all over the place. You can't be law of attraction, history, astronomy and conspiracy theories at the same time. It's bad for marketing if you don't position yourself".* And this is why many world-famous authors sound so bland—they are being told to keep repeating the same stuff without crossover into other fields of knowledge. A few months later another author—I won't say his name - who had copied much of my content into his own book, got the contract with the publisher and the subsequent New York Times Bestseller. I get asked regularly what I think of this author and told how "compatible" his work is with mine. I patiently nod.

Why is there an agenda to keep everyone in their own little us vs. them bubble? Because the anti-human agenda doesn't want people to connect the dots. Normal human behavior is for Christians, Muslims and Jews to sit together and compare their writings. It is not human or normal for them to never sit together, as in modern society. There's a creepy agenda that is keeping them separate. It's normal and human for Government officials to sit with everyday people and get to know their thoughts. Not just for a few weeks while campaigning, but regularly for as long as they are representing them. It is not human-style for Government and populace to be completely alienated from one another, as is the case in our time.

I am proposing discrimination not by race, religion, politics, beliefs but by one thing only: In human interest vs. not in human interest. Many of the things offered in the public square are not in the human interest and we should actively discriminate against them. Is it in human interest for public schools to alienate children from their parents? Is it human-like to dump toxic waste into the local river, visited by your neighborhood? Is it human-style to censor someone whose opinions differ from the mainstream? No? Then we need to actively work to rid ourselves of the most blatant forms of oppression. I can't even blame reptilians for the problems we face. Before any reptilian or evil-doer can gain foothold, we first have to degrade and minimize ourselves by settling for less or by putting up with injustice.

I read a quote saying "The jobs of thousands of government officials depend on no permanent solutions being found for the problems they are paid to work in". That's not a human-made system. It's being allowed because humans have become docile. What made them so docile? Certainly not a pro-human agenda.

As someone who has coached and trained tens of thousands of people in-person I assure you that humans are not docile and apathetic by nature. They are willing and eager to learn, grow, experience, love, give and create when you create a context of freedom. There are authoritarian philosophies according to which "too much freedom" makes a human complacent, spoiled, overwhelmed, etc. Some go so far as to claim it turns them into barbaric animals. This is not my experience at all. They are turned to their lower, animal-self through fear, grief, hate or revenge, not through freedom.

"The science" taught at any university in our day, is that the universe, intelligence, and consciousness are a coincidence without meaning or purpose. This belief-system is void of love or empowerment, it's the "science" of the depressed. The way society is run really points toward a non-human or non-loving influence and presence in our realm. The only remaining question now is whether this alien influence is in fact reptilian. By all "mythological" and "religious" accounts, it certainly is. I've in fact come to suspect that the terms "mythology" and "religion" are reptilian creations to mask that this was simply the knowledge of every day-life, owned by our ancestors. They didn't call it "Religion", it's just the way things were.

"Circular buildings are better for us but are suppressed. Square buildings are not that good for us. Better: Turrets, Domes, Spirals."

Architecture affects consciousness and vice versa. The block-architecture of our days is anti-aesthetic and therefore anti-human. It astonishes me how many people remark "there are so many ugly buildings" but fail to ascend to the next question of "why is that so?" and "what can be done about it?"

On December 23, 2010, after her death, a new book by "Susan Reed" was published, titled "A Conspiracy in the Heavens". Apparently it was material she had already written but not yet put together for a book, because it read jumbled and erratic. As intrigued as I was, I lost interest in finishing the book. It was along the same lines about Reptilians, John of God and the antics of various entities. In this book she claimed that Archangel Michael was a sex addict and rapist who was working with the reptilians and the actual Mary Magdalene was an evil sorceress. From reading the book I realized that Jennifer Gosbell was telling the truth but she couldn't tell that she was being lied to by the various entities that were talking to her. Just because an entity uses the name "Archangel Michael" doesn't mean that this is actually *the* famous Archangel Michael. Another thing I learned from reading the two books is that some of these "Reptilians" are not all that smart. It's surprising that such creatures should have any power over us or our world at all. If real, then their only power comes from our unawareness of them. It's also possible that the book was not written by Jennifer at all, considering it was put out after her death. I learned nothing of interest from the book. May Jennifer Gosbell rest in peace.

By now we've looked at two authors who wrote about Reptilians. Neither of them achieved any fame or fortune, quite the contrary. But both shared knowledge that was later verified. I understand this still does not prove the reality of reptilians, but perhaps you are starting to see that they're worth investigating.

Image: Lindworm statue in Klagenfurt, Austria. Lindwurm or Lindworm is the ancient German name for the Dragon.

4

My Experiences
With The Reptilians

In my childhood I "somehow knew" of Reptilians and their agenda. Then, in my 20s, 30s and 40s the idea faded into the background, into a fog of uninterest and disbelief. In the year I write this book I'm 1 year short of 50 and realize that my child-self may have known more than the adult-self.

I read so much on the topic because I hadn't come to terms with my own Reptilian experiences. I suppressed them into the subconscious, instead of facing them. This book is my way of dealing with childhood trauma around reptilians by confronting the topic head-on. After the book is published, I naturally release my preoccupation with it.

None of the books I read talk about Reptilians invading one's personal experience. The endless conspiracy-literature on the topic, by authors such as David Icke, make it look like Reptilians are residing in Buckingham Palace and the Vatican, rather than targeting every one of us, personally. They fail to teach the spiritual techniques required to win the war against them. This war is first and primarily won at a psychological level, not at Buckingham Palace. The conspiracy books are remarkably shallow when it comes to equipping people with empowering tools. It's almost as if their intention is to sow fear and apathy rather than transcend this ancient adversary. The entities attempt to infiltrate and degrade every aspect of society, so in a later chapter I will go into detail on how we can defeat them.

My first encounters were in childhood. Between the ages 4 and 5 I had vivid "dreams" in which I was harassed, abducted, transported by hostile beings. Some of these had green scales, which I later learned were called Reptilian. Some of them had beautiful luminous scales of different colors even though they were serpents. This is an example of what I earlier called "evil but high vibe". They were incredibly beautiful, "made in Heaven" but nonetheless hostile. It's difficult for the mind to reconcile these two opposites. It's what makes them revered through ancient cultures.

I don't remember the purpose of the visitations, only that a lot of night-time screaming was involved, to the dismay of my parents. One morning, after another of many abduction events, I had markings and bruises on my skin which I didn't recall self-inflicting. I said it was "monsters" who "came out of the closet". The visitations were always accompanied by a low drone or humming sound that gradually increased in volume until the entities arrived through their portal. The entities did not always appear reptilian. Sometimes they had a skin-suit on, looking like humans with but with black eyes. Sometimes they appeared as a human looking man wearing a striped sweater.

At one point, my parents began praying for me. The visitations subsided. My father said he once saw four angels standing around my bed when he got up at night to go to the restroom. They were very tall, shining white beings so glorious he could barely look at them. He quickly went back to bed and fell asleep. After these luminous beings were seen, the Reptilian visitations stopped. Prayers are heard and answered.

My next encounter with Reptilians was in 1984. I was ten years old. Another vivid dream or nightmare. In the dream there was an airplane flying close above my head. It crashed nearby, passengers were shouting in pain and horror. The plane broke in two pieces and caught fire. Behind the scenery there was a giant flying reptile or dragon, responsible for the crash. The dragon was red. Then the dragon turned into a flying saucer. Soon there were thousands of flying saucers in the sky. I woke up and made a drawing of the event. I didn't tell anyone, because it was difficult for me to express why this meant so much to me. The intensity-level of the dream is what makes it relevant. It's not just random, there is a reason I am receiving such dreams at peak-broadcast-intensity. Someone is trying to send me a message, perhaps my own higher self. It could also be reptilians themselves sending me the message. The dream had the "high vibe but evil" quality to it. I think I can sense this energy-field in the world because of my own encounters with these beings. Because they visited me when I was a child, I can spiritually "smell" them.

That dream is reminiscent of the 1984 TV-Series "V" and the 2012 remake.

Needless to say, I've watched both shows in full. I watched the old 1984 version with my dad in 1986, as a twelve-year-old. While watching, I withheld from him, how excited I was about the show. I didn't want him to notice that it was *immensely* important to me. In those days the only important day of the week was when "V" was showing, all else was irrelevant (yes, there was a time we had to wait for a thing to be broadcast, we couldn't just choose to watch whatever we like at any time). The young boy wanted to shout out "This is real! This is the ONLY real thing we've ever watched on TV. This is the ONLY agenda there is and we need to organize and defeat them!". But I kept quiet. I'd steal glances over at him to check whether he was cognizant of how relevant the show is, but to him it was nothing more than the usual entertainment. I remember that he'd normally offer a small bowl of ice-cream when we watched our favorite shows, but when V came on I declined. I was too excited to eat anything. Had I accepted the ice-cream, he'd see that my hands were shaking with excitement. Now that I look back at this, I'm quite surprised I never pursued this line of research as an adult. I must have gotten distracted from my real mission. A 12-year-old kid who is shaking with excitement at such a topic, has obviously found something linked to his life's work. In those days we had a booklet called "TV Guide" that showed us when a show was being broadcast, who directed it, some actors and a short description of the show, just like on Netflix today. Research in the days before Internet wasn't easy, but I made sure to note the name of the director and writer and find out what other shows and movies they made, convinced they were trying to get the truth out.

I watched the 2012 version with my wife and once again, I withheld from her how interested I was in the show. "Did you like it? Would you like us to watch the rest of it together?" Why was I, a grown man in his late thirties, still suppressing my fascination with this? Why was I withholding it from everyone? I don't know. But right now, in 2023, it no longer feels controversial, uncomfortable, strange or even provocative in the slightest. Writing this book comes easily and I have no qualms about publishing it. Is it possible that I kept it to myself because there was a real danger in those days that is no longer there at present?

At the time of my childhood dream about the plane crash, I hadn't seen the TV series yet. The series was made in 1984, but I first watched it years later. So, my dream couldn't have been influenced by it. Unless it was influenced by what I would see in the future (dreams rarely adhere to linear time). Or perhaps I was picking up on what the nation was thinking while watching the series on TV? Or maybe they were seeding the idea into public consciousness and I got it through a dream? It doesn't matter. What matters is that I felt strongly about it. I was only 12 years old and had downloaded ideas about reptilian-alien-invasions, hostile flying saucers appearing as friendly and many other strange things that are not a normal part of a young boys' thoughts. Or perhaps they are normal young-boy thoughts but have been "educated" and "trained" out of people?

It was remarkable how much this meant to me compared to other stuff. The dream was more important to me than school, parents, friends, movies, shows, food, etc. I felt like the reptilian topic was part of my mission. Looking back on my life, I didn't turn it into my mission. I wrote on all kinds of topics but not on reptilians. But I'm doing it now. Better late than never!

Is it possible that there is absolutely nothing to any of this "reptilian stuff" and I've been fed disinformation by strange psychotronic weaponry that beamed dreams and thoughts into my head? Sure. Anything is possible. But this explanation is false. Reptilians are an ancient and enduring part of our history.

My next encounter with the topic happened more than a decade later, in my late twenties. In the meantime, I was living my life as if there were no Reptilians. And honestly, it's easy to live life that way. So easy in fact, that I've wondered whether it really makes a difference whether I write this book. Does life change with the knowledge of reptilians?

Whether Reptilians exist or not, the challenges remain the same—find work, find romance, experience life, etc. Knowing about Reptilians at a surface-level, does not make much of a difference. It might make you a little more resilient when it comes life-success: "If the game is rigged against humans, I'm going to put more effort into being the best I can be, to defy those nasty creatures". But apart from that, I can't think of why it would make a difference whether you eat, drink, sleep and finally die knowing or not knowing about *them*. At least not in a normal state of consciousness. But as you ascend in consciousness, the topic does become relevant because you become aware of the broader, cosmic-games being played. The way the topic makes a real impact on your life is if you personally take responsibility and join the fight to rid our planet of them. That is, if you consciously join the spiritual fight against them on the astral plane, the dreamscape and the celestial realms or become a member of a militia that is actively fighting them. I personally don't know of any such militia but I'm sure they exist. Obviously they wouldn't advertise their existence online.

I was in my late twenties and staying at my girlfriends place over the weekend. We had been together for two years but I was bored with the relationship. Up to that point I hadn't the courage to break-up. Nobody enjoys abandoning another person, but I knew it would benefit us both. I excused myself, saying I'd go for a walk. After ten minutes I came across a small, cozy looking bookshop. I went inside and found the book "Children of the Matrix" by David Icke.

I had never read a book by this author. Before I even opened it, "I knew" what it's about and that every single thing in the book is true (or, at least that's what I thought). I was excited. Much more excited than I had been, lounging around at my girlfriend's house. I got immersed in the book. My being this engrossed and happy about reading on the "forbidden subject", helped me understand I'd been wasting my time in a relationship that had run its course. I'd much rather pursue this line of detective-work than sit on a couch drinking wine and watching some random soap-opera (I'll later learn that, if you found the right partner, you'll gladly watch any random thing with them). I bought the book, went back to the house and ended the relationship. There were tears and hugs. I was sad but much lighter when I left the house. I spent the rest of the day reading the book. I read half of it on the same day and the other half when I woke up the next morning. Again, the sheer excitement, to the point of breaking up a relationship, should have been a pointer toward my life's purpose but I again ignored the call. After the book got shelved, I again forgot about the topic for several years.

Some have stated that reptilians exist in the flesh, not only as astral-entities. I say I've never encountered them in the physical. But maybe it's better to say "not knowingly". They are said to be shapeshifters with the talent to take on human form. Others say there are reptilian human hybrids that look human enough if they hide certain body parts.

I've had encounters strange enough that they could be reptilian. One example of many: A child three years of age was crying in horror. A woman was holding him and greedily licking the sweat off of the child's neck. She looked ecstatic, as if she was getting high off the child's fear. The tongue licking the child's neck had a strange motion to it, like the tongue of a snake. Then the woman looked up and noticed I was watching her. She hadn't known I was in the building, she thought herself alone with the child. When she noticed that I had watched the whole scene she looked like a deer in the headlights. Her face was covered in fear. I said "What are you doing?" and she said "What? So what?". Those were her exact words. "I saw what you were doing" I insisted. She laughed nervously. "I wasn't doing anything". I could tell she was not in the same state she had been previously. I myself felt spooked out by what just happened and quickly left the building without further words. It was one of many encounters that made me *wonder*. What I learned from the incident: They are afraid to be exposed.

Once, in my late twenties, I was conducting coaching with a member of a European royal family, I don't wish to share details. I had gained this contact through a training company I had been working for. Being a reliable and discreet coach, they often sent me to the V.I.P.s before their other staffers.

This person invited me to an island on a lake in mainland Europe. It wasn't her estate, but she had been able to use a part of it for that time. The only way to get there was by ferry. We held our session in the main mansion of the island, in a spacious and beautiful living room that went into a conservatory with glass roofs. I sat on a peach-colored chair made of a velvet-like material. I remember the chair was gigantic, and I looked like a dwarf in it. After three hours I called out a lunch break, during which I took a walk outside, enjoying the views. The break gave both of us time to reflect on our work.

When I returned from outdoors, I opened the door to the beautiful room we had been working in. I couldn't go in because the foulest stench I've *ever* smelled, came out of it. I don't even know what to compare it to… rotting corpses? City sewage? It was too much to handle as I stumbled back and retched. We're not just talking about a toilet smell or the smell of trash. This was something noxious, from the the pits of hell. I stayed outside, catching my breath, confused and horrified. I had never smelled anything that bad and wasn't eager to return to the room. Two minutes later my stomach was still churning with revulsion. While I gasped for fresh air. The smell had been so violently disgusting that my sight blurred for a moment. I had an obligation to finish the coaching, but I didn't want to go back. The coaching had gone well enough. To my amazement, an older man showed up, and informed me that "the consultation" is finished and that the lady had left the island and that "she thanks you for your services". It had never happened to me that a student just disappears mid-session, without saying goodbye. I didn't like it. It felt fake.

"Are you sure? We have five more hours to go" I responded. "Yes, she's quite happy but that will be all. The next ferry is at 2:30 pm". He turned and walked away closing the door behind him. I heard him locking the door as well. A dozen thoughts raced through my mind all at once. "Was the Coaching not good enough? Did it bring up stuff she wasn't willing to face? Did they murder her because they knew she's a Reptilian, before she could harm me? (Yes, my mind gets really creative) Or was she murdered by Reptilians and are they now trying to get rid of me before I find out? You might wonder why my first thoughts were around Reptilians. It's because of the smell. I couldn't imagine anything earthly smelling that way, not even a corpse. The main thing I learned from this event is that if you bring something to planet earth from another density–where it doesn't belong–the smell is too different for the human body to handle. One shouldn't mix realms or densities. For years after the traumatizing event, I had problems dealing with foul smells. I overreacted to them. I'd gag when taking out the trash, had trouble entering public toilets and was horrified of the smell of sewage. I required sessions of emotional clearing to overcome the trauma. I realized I was healed a few months ago. I had accidentally put uneaten fish into the trashcan without wrapping it in anything. The trashcan stood in my garage, unemptied for a week. It was 105 degrees Fahrenheit (40 Celsius) and Humid that week. The next time I entered the garage was two days after I had deposited the old fish there. It was probably the second-worst smell I experienced after the island-event. "Oh my god, no!" I cried, shutting the door behind me. But I held my nose, went back in and removed the trashcan to an outdoor place for further handling. It was doable.

The island event was abrupt. But instead of investigating or protesting, I simply made my way to the ferry station. There were a couple of tourists there, for its beautiful gardens. After the stench, I was relieved not to return to coaching. I was relieved to be heading back home. At the time, I didn't want to know what could have produced such a smell. It's clear to me that what happened produced the smell and also made it impossible to continue the coaching. The lady I had coached with was a polite character. She wouldn't have left the coaching without saying goodbye. After giving it some thought, I knew she enjoyed our session and wouldn't have cut it short. Maybe she got killed. From that point forward, every time someone spoke of the reptilian or the demonic as being associated with foul smells, I listened as someone who had *experienced*. When you watch a horror-movie, you do so from the dissociated comfort of your home, not having to bear the smell, taste and touch of evil. Without these, the monsters on the screen are mere harmless caricatures. But there are real horrors out there and I am grateful that I've been spared looking at or having to touch whatever produced that smell.

My final near-reptilian or possible-reptilian encounter was in my late thirties on an island north of Germany. It's the only event that still brings tears to my eyes when I remember it. I was at a party hosted by a friend of a friend. The friend was a musician trying to land gigs and get record contracts. He believed going to parties would benefit him.

While looking for the restroom, I accidentally stumbled on a couple having sex. I'd have to put "couple" and "sex" into quotation marks. It's one of the most dehumanizing, dispiriting things I've ever seen. The man was pounding down on an unconscious or now dead woman like a jackhammer. It was unhuman, machine-like. Her head sometimes bumped against the wall, but he didn't take notice. There is no pornography where a human being pounds into another with such speed and violence. I saw them from the side. The woman's head was rolling left and right as if she were a doll. She had long lost consciousness or maybe she had been raped to death by this creature. The "mans" face was a psychotic grimace and his eyes were glowing yellow. I remember being so shocked by the eyes that I quickly scurried away. I had lost all interest in the party, the people or socializing. I just wanted to get as far away from that house as possible. My "reasoning" mind later said that the yellow eyes must have been a reflection of some light or the guy must have been wearing weird lenses. I was trying to tell myself that I didn't see what I saw. I was telling myself that I didn't see him at the best angle. I had also had some alcohol, so I shouldn't judge what I saw. And surely the woman was merely unconscious, not dead. And the guy was just into rough sex, nothing unhuman about it. But upon reflection, while writing this book, I realize that I've been making excuses and rationalizing *outrageous evil* too often. If I'm going to write a good book on Reptilians, I need to view things as they are. And that event was an absolute horror-show. I don't know if he killed the girl or not, but by the way he was "making love" you could tell it didn't matter to him. And that's the attitude of an entity that's hostile to humanity. If I'd see the same scene today, I'd intervene. In those days I was too weak, mentally and physically.

From that particular scene, I understand why people would rather put their head in the sand and live in denial that evil even exists. Nobody wants to see what these creatures are capable of and what they've done to humans.

I have had other personal encounters with psychopaths. I've seen and witnessed people behaving in manners hostile to human nature. I'm not going to elaborate because I wish to limit graphic details of evil to only a few examples. Enough to make the point but not so much to turn this book itself into a lower-vibratory frequency.

Even if Reptilians didn't exist, a widespread agenda hostile to the native *loving kindness* of humans, does exist. From the way our supermarkets are laid out to how the pharmaceutical industry or news-media operate, it's obvious to me that "they" despise human beings. And if they despise human beings, they are probably not themselves humans. That's just logical deduction.

Have you noticed how every genuine, legitimate, positive movement has a counterfeit shadow at lower consciousness?

Genuine Movements
vs. Counterfeit Diversions

Legitimate political and spiritual movements are often diverted to something lesser. For everything real and positive a human creates, a counterfeit is created by lower consciousness. Examples below.

Genuine   Diverted

Environmental   Climate Change
Protection   Propaganda

Women's Rights   Man-Hating
Movement   Ideology

National Self-Interest   Oppressing
                              Foreign Countries

Advances of   Big-Pharma
Modern Medicine   Corruption

Spirituality   Fanaticism

It is as if a dark agenda takes everything positive and turns it foul. If the Reptilians are real, we must first look at what our ancestors said about who is running the show on Earth. And there we find, across all cultures, all of "mythology", all of religion a reptilian entity, referred to as the snake, the serpent, the nagas, the dragons.

Did you know there were even Dragons in Heaven? Most people don't know this, it's something the religious omit or fail to mention because it does not fit their simplistic view of Heaven. They learn Heaven = good and Serpent = Bad. But if the serpent, the dragon or Satan is a "fallen angel" he'd have had to first be in Heaven. The Bible makes several references to angelic beings called Seraphim. For example, in Isaiah 6:2–6, the prophet Isaiah speaks of what he saw in Heaven and says:

Above it stood seraphim; each one had six wings: with two he covered his face, with two he covered his feet, and with two he flew.

The word seraph or saraph is translated as "angel", but the Hebrew root of the word means fiery serpent. We learn that some of these fiery serpents became "fallen angels" who despised humankind and proceeded to become the illegitimate rulers of Earth. When I was younger, this was nothing more than a story to me. Maybe true, maybe not. But the more I know, the more I realize that it's probably the best explanation for everything that's been happening under the sun.

Image: The Aztec serpent-God Quetzalcoatl shown as an upright walking reptilian.

5

The Disappearance
Of Arizona Wilder

People who go public with personal experiences about Reptilians tend to disappear under mysterious circumstances. This element of Reptilian-research lends credence to the field. Jenny Gosbell (Susan Reed) disappeared suddenly and so did Arizona Wilder. A skeptic reiterates that "maybe they were embarrassed by their lies, that's why they are hiding from public". If that were true we wouldn't see the high death-count we do in "conspiracy theorists". And it almost always happens to fairly unknown authors of obscure books, right before their reader or follower-count goes above a critical mass. A good example of this is an author by the name of Tracy Twyman, who wrote on occultism. Then, around 2018 this author diverged from her previous topic and started looking into pizzagate. She teamed up with an actor by the name of Isaac Kappy and their horrific discoveries in Arizona were starting to go viral. Shortly thereafter, both were found dead by "suicide". Finally, the whole thing going on in Arizona was hushed up and never saw the light of day.

Between 1999 and 2001 Arizona Wilder gave several public lectures and interviews about MKUltra and Reptilians, a Luciferian Government, Human Experimentation and the governmental exploitation of psychic children. Some of her interview transcripts and lectures can be found online so there is no need for me to reprint them. I will only mention parts of her testimony, relevant to my research.

After 2001 she abruptly stopped giving lectures. A bizarre letter was published online, in what was claimed to be her real name–Jennifer Ann Kealy, retracting her previous revelations. She claimed she had been misled and "programmed" to conduct her most famous interview with David Icke, titled "Revelations of a Mother Goddess". She published her retraction along with a request for donations because she claimed to have to pay ransom money to someone. Later, even more strangely, she disowned the site that had published these retractions, while confirming the information on them:

"This is Jennifer Ann Kealey a.k.a. Arizona Wilder. I was just told about this site. WHO authorized this site? WHO answers questions and comments as if they are coming from me? Jennifer Ann Greene was my married name before I legally changed it to Arizona Wilder because I had been programmed to do so. Only I and the perpetrators could know this, so who/whomever is doing this is a fraud, and was not authorized to do so. I no longer (for many years) condone the use of material I made while involuntarily programmed especially for the David Icke video. His material is not today and has never been my experience nor was the concept of "shape-shifting reptilians" something that I experienced as an unwilling victim at rituals. I was programmed specifically for David Icke's interview as well as the following Conspiracy Con meeting in San Jose, CA. etc., and David Icke as well as Brian Desborough both knew that I had been programmed to respond this way when they made the video. In fact, the ring shown in the video was used to certify to Brian Desborough and David Icke that I had been programmed with preset answers and was to be used for this video."

All the public knows is this:

1. Arizona Wilder speaks of being in recovery from reptilian mkultra programs.
2. Arizona Wilder retracts what she said on a website, claiming she was mkultra programmed to say so.
3. Arizona Wilder disowns the retracting website, claiming someone is playing mkultra tricks on her.

The contradictory statements are evidence that she is mentally not well and/or her mind has been tampered with. Her sudden disappearance after this is evidence that she may have been telling the truth.

The following are mere excerpts from a much longer interview. I have omitted much, including gruesome details around child-abuse, torture and murder. I don't want any of that in my book. But if you're reading this, you already know about all that.

"...And I was talking about ritual abuse issues at the time. And I didn't have the whole thing put together. It's taken me all these years, it's taken approximately almost 10 years, to put together what has happened to me...

And it was because of the bloodline of my mother's family, which comes down through Ireland, but before that it began in France. It was through the Marquis de Staque, which he came to Ireland, and changed the name to Stack, and then I was chosen. The birth was planned. My parents were forced to move down to this area for the reason that the High Council is down here. There are 6 councils of 13 in this country. And the High Council is down here.

...from the time that I was a baby, I was being abused and traumatized on purpose, for the mind control that they need someone to go through to do whatever they say, as just a puppet, that they can control every move. And you don't remember. I didn't remember a lot of things, because I have, as a result of all of this mind control, split off many parts that all hold memories, hold feelings, hold programs, hold information.

"...the Aryans, and the purity of the blood. And what it's all about is that the blood, and the menstrual blood, contains something that is important for the propagation of this race that is controlling things on this planet. And these people that are in the organization, that the Council of 13 is under, and they have something called the Grand Druid Council, or the Octagon. They are called the Illuminati. And the Illuminati are actually run by these 13 bloodlines, which are all of the royal families in Europe, and in England. And they need the blood, because they are in fact not human. They take human shape. They are reptilians. And they need the blood. The blood helps them maintain their reptilian shape. And it helps them maintain their sanity. And it helps them to live in this world, because they are not from this world.

The blood has something in it. It has secretions from the pituitary gland and from the pineal gland, and it has a very strong drug in it. This is the one that keeps them from going crazy. And it's like heroin, or like endorphins. And it's much stronger. But what they need for it to be secreted in the blood, is they need terrorization of their victims before they are killed for their blood. Or if a young woman is beginning to menstruate, they need the menstrual blood. And they have to terrorize them to get this to come out in the blood, and be secreted in the blood.

Yes, that, and this other element comes and secretes out through the blood. This all comes out through the blood at that time. And it's at that point they are actually staring into the eyes, of the head of it, at some of these rituals, or at a reptilian, they are staring into the eyes of, this person. And it's a hypnotic gaze these reptilians have, and it holds the victim in an absolute trance, and a trance of terror. And then they are killed at that moment as they are staring into their eyes. And they can't hold their shape when this happens.

The human shape they cannot hold. They go back into reptilian shape as this is happening, because it's like an animalistic type of excitement of the kill. And often times, they will just rip into the victim, and eviscerate them, and start eating the flesh of this person too. And the fat from the intestinal areas is highly valued, as they use it on their skin. And they drink the blood. And the blood is highly sought after. And it goes also according to rank within these creatures, as to who gets what when. And their sacrifices, it started increasing in the early 80s. The amount that they were doing, is increased. And they use a lot of Druidic holidays to do this. But they have other days too. They've mixed all of these satanic, and what are called satanic holidays and Druidic holidays, in order to have these rituals; which, ritual seems to be important to them. But they also use it in order to drink this blood; that they seem to need more.

…human beings through the ages have accepted gods interbreeding, or being accepted as humans.

In the Illuminati this is important. And it is important to think that about the head of the Illuminati, because what comes from a golden phallus would be a superior seed for a race. And this is what they are doing with all of these bloodlines to keep the bloodlines going, [they] are impregnating people of Aryan blood, that hold high stations with them, impregnating them with this seed of Pindar.

They don't seem to have the psychic abilities. And they look for people that have that. People in the blood line that have that. And I've had a tremendous amount of psychic ability. And so, I was picked and bred from before birth. And this is also something that other survivors that have been in high positions have known about me, and told me.

…they needed the psychic abilities because they control, or attempt to control, events. Because I would have the ability to foretell what was going to happen. And they needed the information to try to control it to an outcome that was good for them. The second thing is that during the rituals, you had to have psychic ability. You have to be very powerful in that way to call out the old ones, that are also reptilian, that come from another dimension. They actually materialize from out of another dimension, and are present at rituals. And they are so powerful, and their presence, there's such an evilness about them, that they want out of this other dimension. And they have to be called out by someone who has that power. And the reptilians don't have this

power. That's very important. They don't have this power to call out these old ones that have to do with them.

We have the ability to foresee, to be able to become vibrationally higher, and see into those levels, go into those levels. And in fact, agencies use this, they call it remote viewing. Humans have the ability to go into the past, go into the future, to go to other places, to astrally leave their body, and to see things. We've always had this ability, and it's like having a third eye, which they don't have. They don't have this ability. So, during ritual, these old ones are called out, and they are what Christianity would have called the demons. They are called out, and there is a circle that has a hexagon in there, which is a powerful occultic symbol, and then there is a pentagram. And then in the middle of that there is a triangle. And if you're the one calling them out, then you stand in the triangle so that you're not devoured or taken by these creatures that come out.

…they cannot get outside the pentagram. And they want out. They are always demanding to be let out. And so, you have to be very powerful to keep them in line, and to make them go back, when it is time for them to go back.

(Reptilians want to manifest these demons at rituals because) It brings power to the rituals. They are told things by these entities, and they are encouraged to go on with what they are doing, and knowledge is imparted to them through these entities. But it takes a person with the ability to bring them out and make them answer, because they don't want to cooperate. They have to cooperate when the right person has control over them.

They have been thrown into that dimension, and they can't leave that dimension. And that's actually what the abyss is about, is being in a different dimension. It's like something to do with the fourth dimension. And before I even knew, for example, what I was saying, or realized what I was saying, I would be saying things to my therapist and other survivors that the fourth dimension was a dimension to stay away from; not at that time understanding the whole thing.

Because the moon has an influence on this planet, and also the sun. These also take place during things that go on with the sun. But the moon, it's kind of a really very cyclical thing with the moon. It takes place on full moons, new moons, it has to do with the current religion, that they are using the druid religion that they've taken and used. They still hold on to the Egyptology type of religion. They hold on to the Druidism though, and they're currently calling themselves Druidic, or Druid. And Druidism is tied in with the cycles of the moon, which, it has to do with planting, sowing, and harvesting. And there are so many days they can use from this, to their own purpose and their own end, that they bring it about"

Arizona Wilder revealed much more than this, but I believe I've captured the gist of her view of the Reptilian Agenda. From all I've learned, I get the sense that they are trapped in a lower realm and desperately seek out humans for blood, flesh, energy and psychic abilities. Their primary agenda is human harvesting. What do we know about human harvesting? Next to nothing.

In my book "Clearing Entities" I've addressed some of the energy-harvesting of these beings and people. Ways and methods to combat these entities on the spiritual plane have already been shared in that book to some extent, but we could use much more research in this field.

Image: Echidna, a reptilian-human hybrid of ancient Greek "Mythology".

6

The Human Meat Conspiracy

"The best way to keep a prisoner from escaping is to make sure he never knows he's in prison." — Fyodor Dostoyevksy

This chapter examines the possibility and feasibility of exploiting humans for flesh and blood. If Reptilians are real and they are what self-proclaimed witnesses tell us, then there is some kind of covert human farming and harvesting going on.

What do you know about human harvesting? Probably not much. It's the one "conspiracy-theory" that isn't broadcast all over the Internet.

A cow happily grazes on rolling green hills under small fluffy clouds. The sun is gentle. It enjoys the breeze, smell of the grass, sound of the birds and the presence of family. Is there any use in telling the cow it will be slaughtered and eaten by its human keepers? What changes? Nothing, except that the happy cow becomes an unhappy cow.

Is it better to withhold the truth? Or should I reveal it, so that the cow has a chance to escape the farmlands and find freedom? But what if the cow concludes there is nothing they can do to escape and continues to stay at the farm? Or if they attempt to escape but are forcefully herded back in line? Or what if all the cows gather and trample their owners to death—only to be violently put down by other humans? Considering that, maybe it really is better to let them live happily until they pass away and serve as nourishment for humans while their souls rest in peace. Some consider human's being eaten part of the natural food chain. But the Abrahamic religion assures us that humans are not meant to be eaten like animals because they are imbued with a higher consciousness, so it's probably not right to make a direct comparison.

Maybe the cows could escape deep into the woods, where humans have not penetrated. There, they could organize and teach their children autonomy. Then, one day, they could achieve liberation for their species and find the next higher version of their existence.

What would you choose, blissful ignorance or truth?

I'd always choose truth. Knowing the reality of my situation may not make me happy but it allows me to make informed decisions. If I know my captors don't have my best interests at heart, I will stop wasting my time trying to gain their approval. I may not escape in my lifetime but I can sow a seed in my children for a future generation to live in freedom.

A human meat-market has been with us for hundreds, if not thousands of years. A quote from the book "Aboriginal Men of High Degree" by anthropologist A.P. Elkin:

"Some of the Tibetan occultists are also believed to practice ritual cannibalism, but in esoteric teaching this is associated with a doctrine of transubstantiation. Some human beings "have attained such high degree of spiritual perfection that the original material substance of their bodies has been transmuted into a more subtle one which possesses special qualities. A morsel of their transformed flesh, when eaten, will produce a special kind of ecstasy and bestow knowledge and supernatural powers upon the person partaking of it." So it is with the Aboriginal postulant in some regions. He partakes of the

corpse and in a mystic way sees the dead or visits the sky, thus deriving power and knowledge,"

Rumour is, that even today, there's an *organized human-meat market,* operated out of warehouses, catering to the rich and powerful. It is claimed this faction of the elite are into occult ritual abuse, forcible rape, murder and cannibalism for energy-parasitism. It's also about *fear-and-trauma based mind-control* (also known as mk-ultra and monarch programming) and mass-attention-harvesting. And it's about the same ruling elite secretly adding human meat to their fast foods and processed foods to get the general populace to unconsciously participate. So far, I've only come across one book that describes the warehouses and human-meat-business in great detail. The book is titled "Blood-Drinking, Cannibalism and High Adept Satanism" and is authored by Kerth Barker–yet another independent author who has meanwhile mysteriously disappeared.

The book was published in 2015, approximately one year prior to the "pizzagate" stuff going public but foreshadows much of what was later learned. I read it in 2016 and followed the author until he abruptly stopped posting videos and publishing books around 2020. This is merely one of thousands of examples of researchers in this topic vanishing without a trace. I am not going to go into anything said in the book here, except to say that in one chapter, there is the implication that some of the cannibalistic elite are "possessed by reptilian spirits".

In attempting to collect research on the topic, I posted inquiries on the "human meat" issue to various well-known discussion-forums on the Internet. The topic got removed on all four forums. Two of these were "conspiracy theory" oriented forums but even there the topic is off-limits. If the inquiries hadn't been censored, I wouldn't have gone ahead with this chapter. The fact of *censorship* not from one or two but four places on the Internet, means there is something worth investigating. An important fact of human psychology is this: untrue and unimportant things are not censored. The internet is full of nonsense conspiracy-theories that can be shared freely. If something is censored, it is always because someone feels threatened by it. But have you ever felt threatened by something that has no basis in reality? Of course not. Of course one could argue that things like "pizzagate", according to which our political and Hollywood elite are engaged in sexual child abuse, cannibalism and murder, are malicious lies, meant to slander and radicalize people. But if that were the case, lawsuits could be filed. Slander and libel are crimes. The fact that those accused in the pizzagate context haven't filed lawsuits and have instead opted to call the whole thing "a debunked conspiracy theory" speaks volumes. Those who consider it "debunked" haven't done the slightest amount of research.

AWARD WINNING ABC JOURNALIST WHO "DEBUNKED" PIZZAGATE, PLEADS GUILTY IN HORRIFIC CHILD PORN CASE.

It was around 2003 I first became acquainted with the idea that human meat was served to "people" who consider themselves "higher up" on the food chain and that there is a secret and elitist human-meat industry. Some among the "rich and famous" dine on human meat and get a kick out of keeping it a secret. They can't help but spill the truth sometimes. I am reminded of when Hollywood actors Adam Sandler and Jennifer Aniston were being interviewed and Sandler started "jokingly" hinting at rape, human sacrifice and cannibal parties and Aniston telling Sandler, live on Camera, "shut your trap!". I've collected hundreds of strange little "leaks" like this. But the truth is so horrific and outrageous that you can tell people directly and they still won't believe it. You can provide extensive documentation, as in this chapter, and they *still* deny it! The cognitive discomfort is just too great. As of today, there is little chance the public will ever find out because people can easily block what they *don't want to see.* Human meat and blood are a high-demand commodity on planet earth. People pay a lot of money for it.

I've had this joke that I've been telling vegetarians over the last 20 years, to tease them:

Animals eat Plants.

Humans eat Animals.

And Extraterrestrials eat Humans.

Little did they know, that I wasn't joking. In eating humans, our "ruling elite" are following the "old religions" that are still practiced among what we call "the indigenous tribes". And these old religions were copying the behaviours of "the gods", non-terrestrial beings who ate humans like we eat cattle. In so doing, they wish to "become like the gods".

I am suggesting, in this chapter, that you are food to the ruling elite. They believe that, to experience power over you, they must eat you. It proves their superiority on the food chain. They have no second thoughts about this, just like most of you have no second thoughts about eating animal meat. One might argue that our cruelty of eating animals is equivalent to theirs, but there is a radical difference. According to most ancient traditions, our Creator decreed that we eat certain animals because *that's what they were created for.* It is their purpose to be eaten. Thus, they're imbued with low consciousness. It is a transgression of the highest order to eat beings with high consciousness, because their purpose is more than to serve as mere meat. Most of you feel queasy eating a dog or cat— that's because these animals are *not meant* to be eaten, they were created to be *companions* to humans. The ruling elite ignore the rules of this realm, because they hate its Creator. And they hate the Creators favourite Creation: Human Beings. So, they use humans as slave labour, for sexual exploitation and as meat. To them, we are nothing more than goods to be trafficked, bought, sold, used and consumed.

From their perspective, "life on Earth" is a farm. Humans are bred and harvested as food, for sex, as slave labour, for energy and as entertainment for the non-human ruling elite.

There is a reason we are ignorant of most everything. Or would you teach the cow that you are going to eat, the skills it needs to become independent?

Keep in mind that I am not claiming that this is the primary purpose of our planet and realm. We are divinely created beings who were created to tend to and garden planet Earth while growing spiritually in a denser realm. Planet Earth being exploited for gain by other beings is only one of many games going on.

Like vampires, they also drink the blood of humans. Like cannibals, they eat their flesh. I've heard claims of slave labour camps in remote areas of the earth, in subterranean caverns and even off-world. Human beings are abducted and raped at every age. Their skin is used to make boots, shoes, bags and other leather products. Their fat is used in beauty products. Their excrement is used as fertilizer. Their meat is used in fast-food chains such as McDonalds. Does it sound utterly outrageous to you that McDonalds would serve human meat? Or does it sound like science-fiction to you that humans are abducted as slave labour to other worlds outside of earth? Well, let's see if we find *evidence* for any of this.

Has it ever occurred to you that McDonalds serves much more meat than cattle available? And is that because McDonalds processes human meat? If true, would a company like McDonalds benefit from war, because it means more and cheaper meat?

My *first* hint about there being something "not quite right" about McDonalds was the fact that endless "fact checkers" claim that McDonalds *doesn't* serve human meat. I never suspected McDonalds would do anything that nefarious, but when they *kept denying a thing, we never accused them of,* I got suspicious. It never occurred to me that they process human meat, but they made the mistake of putting attention on the topic by denying it just a little too often.

Here's an example of one of the "fact checks" posted on Yahoo News, quoting USA Today. Pay close attention (bolding mine):

"The claim: McDonald's closed in three countries for serving human meat; worldwide closures soon.

Health experts have long been concerned about the health impact of food from McDonald's. But a post on social media claims the fast-food chain's ingredients are more nefarious than expected.

"BOOM McDonalds closed in 3 countries for serving human meat...!!!" reads a Dec. 27 Facebook post. "Worldwide closure soon."

The post received more than 100 reactions and shares in two days.

But it's not true. The false claim that human meat is served by McDonald's has circulated online since 2014, when it was first shared by a satire site. **McDonald's debunked the claim on its website.**

USA TODAY reached out to the Facebook user who shared the claim for comment.

No human meat in McDonald's' food

In response to a question in the "Your Right to Know" section of its website, **McDonald's debunked the claim.**

"We do not have any human meat in our burgers," the fast-food company's answer reads. "We would like to assure you that we only use 100% pure, Halal beef and chicken in our food. That's it!"

The answer also says that McDonald's sources its beef from Brazil Foods in Abu Dhabi and chicken from McFood in Malaysia.

Iterations of the claim have circulated online since 2014, when the website Huzlers shared a post headlined "McDonalds Exposed For Using Human Meat!"

But the article is satire. The website describes itself as a "satirical and fictional entertainment blog." Under the post author's byline is the tagline "Believe half of what you see and nothing you read online."

The Facebook post is an example of what might be called "stolen satire," in which made-up claims published and labeled as satire are captured via screenshot and reposted in a way that makes them appear to be legitimate news. As a result, readers of the second-generation post are misled, as was the case here.

McDonald's declined to comment on the claim.

Our rating: False

Based on our research, we rate FALSE the claim that McDonald's closed in three countries for serving human meat and worldwide closures are soon to come. The false claim that human meat is served by McDonald's has circulated online since 2014, when it was first shared by a satire site. ***McDonald's debunked the claim on its website"***

Source: https://news.yahoo.com/fact-check-no-mcdonalds-doesnt-163314311.html

The state of journalism is so bad that when you read any article in USA Today, you feel you are talking to a grade-school student. Three times the author assures us that "McDonalds debunked this!".

But that's not how reality works. The source that is being *accused* cannot be the *same* source *debunking* the accusation. Genuine debunking must come from an uninvolved *neutral party*. The notion that McDonalds debunks that they did anything wrong, requires a childlike naivety that modern "journalism" expects of the reader. Just how dumb are these "fact checkers"? And how stupid do they think their readership is? Do they think their readership will just nod and say "oh OK, McDonalds debunked it. Obviously, if McDonalds says all is well, there is nothing to see here".

But would McDonalds PR Department say anything *other* than what they said? I don't think anyone would openly admit to serving human meat in a restaurant.

Yes, of course there are a lot of satire sites out there, talking about human meat. And a lot of trashy sites that make this particular line of thinking look stupid. That's a routine part of their cover-up. Fortunately, cannibalism actually lowers a person's intelligence, so their cover-ups are easily blown apart.

If you search on McDonalds and human meat, the first three pages of Google are "fact checkers" doing their "debunking" and the "satire article". But if you dig a little more patiently or use other, independent search engines (the purpose of Google is to censor the truth), you quickly find more.

Here's an article-snippet from Fortune Magazine:

Analysis of Burger Market Finds Unwanted Ingredients: Rat and Human DNA

The most unappetizing results of a recent test of 258 burgers at their molecular level found three instances in which the meat contained rat DNA and one in which human DNA was found.

Bay Area-based startup Clear Labs, which conducted the analysis, notes that while unpleasant, human and rat DNA are not likely to be harmful to human health…

Clear Labs selected the burgers from retailers and fast-food chains in northern California in order to provide a representative sampling of the burger market, including vegetarian and other non-beef varieties. The burgers covered 79 brands from 22 retailers and included ground meat and frozen patties. The company says it does not call out any of the specific brands or retailers because it's not a consumer watchdog organization and has developed its technology alongside the food industry.

Source: https://fortune.com/2016/05/10/burger-market-analysis-rat-human-dna/

It's surprising any independent party would check McDonalds for traces of human meat. Who gets such an idea? We are lucky to have scientists discovering human DNA among McDonalds products.

"Traces of human DNA" is not proof that the Burgers are made of human meat. I realize these traces may have been accidental. More testing is needed.

Why are Burgers called Burgers? That's the German word for "citizens" and "people". Why would you want to eat something called "people"? Even stranger is that McDonald's, Burger King and all the others didn't change the name of their Burgers in German-speaking countries.

Human teeth, fingers, toes, eyeballs, tongues, noses and entrails are routinely found in fast-food restaurants, to the utter disgust of their guests. I've chosen not to quote the hundreds of relevant news articles here because it's not necessary to go into ghastly detail. The news articles make these incidents out to be accidental. They'll claim, for instance, that an employee cut off his finger without noticing it. How can you chop off your finger and not notice? Again, the level of "journalism" out there is just so bad it makes being a flesh-eating villain easy. An example:

In 2006, an Indiana diner found a finger on his TGI Friday's burger after a restaurant employee accidentally cut it in the kitchen, according to an AP story at the time. "The manager didn't even know it happened until he got to the hospital," the TGI Friday's spokeswoman said.

Source: https://www.npr.org/sections/thetwo-way/2012/05/17/152923061/a-history-of-human-fingers-found-in-fast-food

It's the sheer stupidity of the articles that are the head-scratcher to me. *"He didn't know he cut his finger until he got to the hospital"*. If he didn't know he cut his finger, why did he go to the hospital?

You'll see this kind of writing a lot when it comes to this topic. There's journalistic laziness because the people writing it are not journalists, they are shills. Thugs posing as journalists. Criminals struggle with logic and reason, so they put out articles that make no sense. The article above was posted to NPR which is partially funded by the Government.

In many cases the restaurant owners categorically deny that the body parts come from their own employees. An example (bolding mine):

*A Japanese woman got more than a mouthful when she discovered fragments later identified as "dental material" in a McDonald's hamburger, marking the fast-food chain's latest food quality embarrassment. The news, confirmed by McDonald's on Friday, comes two days after the company admitted **several foreign objects had been found in food at Japanese outlets**, including a human tooth in a container of french fries at an outlet in Osaka.*

*An unidentified woman told the Asahi television network she had found three tiny fragments of what looked like teeth in a burger she bought at a McDonald's in northern Kushiro city in September. "I took a bite and there was a crunch," the woman said in footage aired Friday, adding that she initially thought it was a piece of sand or stone. **"I can't help thinking that it was (already) in the meat."***

A third-party examination determined the opaque white fragments were "dental material", according to company spokeswoman Miwa Yamamoto, saying the substance is commonly used to fill cavities or in other dental work. McDonald's, however, would not confirm the woman's claim that the fragments were inside her burger.

*Yamamoto said the customer was told that there was an "extremely low chance" it could have fallen into raw material, given the highly-mechanised process. **None of the employees at the outlet had issues with their teeth at the time** and the customer denied it could have come from her, Yamamoto said.*

Source: https://food.ndtv.com/food-drinks/woman-finds-dental-material-in-japan-mcdonalds-burger-724907

The news items so far could be put off as unlucky coincidences. They don't prove a human meat industry. So let's get to the meat of the matter, shall we?

*Joe Metheny is a serial killer who took 10 lives in the 1990s. He was nicknamed "The Cannibal Killer" because he opened a meat stand during his spree and **served human meat mixed with pork**.*

Whether his customers ever figured out what they actually ate is unknown.

Source: https://www.ranker.com/list/unintentional-cannibals/katherine-ripley

The mixing of pork with human meat is fairly common among front restaurants run by organized crime, because pork and human meat don't taste different from each other. You may be surprised to hear this, but it's common knowledge in some circles.

Some say this is the true reason religions prohibit the eating of pork—to prevent the secret mixing of the two.

According to the Daily Mail, in 2011, a Russian chef took the life of his father-in-law after an argument, and then used meat from his remains to make pies, which he served to customers in a popular cafe.

Neither the suspect nor the cafe was named, but it was located about two miles from the Kremlin. Apparently, dozens of pies were sold before police figured out what the chef had put in them.

Source: https://www.ranker.com/list/unintentional-cannibals/katherine-ripley

Serving human meat to your fellow humans is truly anti-human. I have difficulty believing that any human being would do this, even if they hated me. Such people are either possessed by non-human entities, or they're reptilian hybrids, or both.

Nathaniel Bar-Jonah was a serial killer who allegedly served the meat of a 10-year-old boy to guests at a neighborhood barbecue.

He was eventually sentenced to 130 years in prison for multiple crimes.

Source: https://www.ranker.com/list/unintentional-cannibals/katherine-ripley

I am only sharing very small snippets from longer stories in this book. Digging deeper into either of these, often reveals links to organized crime, occultism and big money. Why occultism? Because eating human flesh has to do with discarnate entities.

In 2014, the Daily Mail published a story about human meat being served by two brothers in Quetta, one of the largest cities in Pakistan. Apparently, people began to realize that something was wrong when they smelled odd odors coming from their home.

The brothers had been robbing graves and using the meat from human remains in their curries. They were arrested, and Pakistan officially outlawed cannibalism following the scandal.

https://www.ranker.com/list/unintentional-cannibals/katherine-ripley

A deeper look into this story revealed that they had been running their "curry" Business for 10 years. It took that long before the unsuspecting public caught on to them!

Zhang Yongming is a Chinese serial killer who carved flesh from his victims' bodies and sold it in a market as "ostrich meat."

This incident occurred several years after he was released from prison, where he had been serving time for murder.

Source: https://www.ranker.com/list/unintentional-cannibals/katherine-ripley

*Jorge Beltrao Negromonte is a serial killer who, with help from his wife and other women **in their cult**, baked his victims into pies and sold them on the streets of Guaranhuns, Brazil, where he lived.*

The local police chief was apparently a big fan of the pies, but when he found out what Negromonte and his wife were doing, instead of arresting them, he let them leave in exchange for their property. Negromonte wasn't arrested until after he claimed two more lives in another city.

Source: https://www.ranker.com/list/unintentional-cannibals/katherine-ripley

A common feature of cannibals, even though not mentioned in many news-stories, is their membership in all sorts of strange "cults", "clubs", "circles", "covens", "brotherhoods" and "rings". I mentioned it earlier and bring it up again because it's curiously omitted from mainstream articles. It would trouble the people if they knew these are not the works of lone whackos but of highly organized and well-funded groups.

*Leonarda Cianciulli was a mentally disturbed Italian woman who became convinced that in order **to keep her son safe** when he went off to fight in WWII, **she had to perform human sacrifices**. She took the lives of three women and used their blood to make tea cakes, which she served to her friends when they came to visit.*

She also used flesh from one of her victims to make "some most acceptable creamy soap," which she gave away to neighbors.

Source: Source: https://www.ranker.com/list/unintentional-cannibals/katherine-ripley

Entity-influence keeps revealing itself in the common belief of a reward for committing anti-human acts.

You'll have noticed I use the word "anti-human" a lot, instead of criminal, atrocious, horrible, etc. This is because, if we look at the issues coldly, neutrally, with the eyes of a scientist, what it all comes down to is anti-human sentiment. I use the word to build an awareness that the real enemy is not our fellow human. They are not the Chinese, not white people, not blacks, not jews, not the Russians. They are anti-human, against humanity.

As for the humans in these news-stories, I believe they are under un-human influence. I am not saying that humans play no part in evil. To come under the influence of negative entities, one would first have to make a lot of really bad choices in life. As humans we are ultimately responsible for our actions, regardless of whether we are under strange influence.

Nikolai Dzhumagaliev was a serial killer who lived in the Soviet Union and took the lives of escorts. Apparently, he liked to use his victims to cook ethnic dishes and then serve them to his friends at parties.

One night he gave himself away when he invited two people over to his house for dinner, and they discovered a human head and intestines in the refrigerator.

Source: https://www.ranker.com/list/unintentional-cannibals/katherine-ripley

*Enriqueta Martí was a female serial killer who lived in Spain in the late 19th century. She was also **a practicing witch doctor**. She would kidnap and slay street children, and then use their remains to make foods and medicines that she would sell on the black market.*

It's unclear whether her wealthy customers knew exactly what they were buying. Authorities never figured out who Martí's clients were because she was lynched in prison before she was tried.

Source: https://www.ranker.com/list/unintentional-cannibals/katherine-ripley

I share these news-items to increase an awareness that "human meat" is a thing. Practitioners of what is nowadays called "witchcraft" follow ways of some indigenous people according to which the blood and flesh of humans contains the person's life force, making the eater more powerful, healthy and young. This is what's really behind the "infusion of young blood" industry and old hags hanging around playgrounds trying to siphon energy off kids. Integrous old people view children with joy and laughter. The non-integrous view the exuberance of children as something to vampirize. I don't want to go into too much detail but if you have children, I recommend you accompany them to playgrounds. And if you see shady people hanging around playgrounds, I recommend you confront them.

I used to play tennis beside a certain playground. Apart from other tennis players and a lot of children, there were always certain grim and creepy looking folk, with unkempt, greasy hair and dead eyes. What were they doing staring at the children? As I easily saw from the tennis court, they didn't have children of their own at the playground. What Business do they have there? They were like peeping toms. This is all to do with energy-vampirism because lower-astral entities lack energy and power.

Police in Anambra, Nigeria have arrested 11 people, including the owner of a restaurant, in connection with selling human meat.

According to the article in a Nigerian publication the police recovered at least two fresh human heads when they arrested 11 people from the restaurant including the owner, six women and four men, following a tip-off.

The blood-soaked heads were found wrapped in cellophane.

Officials have also seized two AK-47 rifles, other weapons, dozens of rounds of ammunitions and several mobile phones during the raid.

The un-named restaurant is in a hotel located close to the Ose-Okwodu market in Anambra state.

One witness account spoke of suspicious movements in and around the hotel and market.

Another outraged unidentified pastor could not believe the price they were selling the meat at after eating at the hotel.

Source: https://www.food24.com/nigerian-restaurant-shut-down-for-serving-human-meat/

News source Asia One reported about a vegetarian restaurant in Bangkok serving dishes that included human flesh. Thai police have confirmed that the victim was Prasit Inpathom, a 61-year-old who had been reported missing and was found dead in a septic tank on October 23rd.

The restaurant owner was found out after patrons complained about bits of meat in their vegetarian dishes.

Source: https://1059thebrew.iheart.com/content/2018-11-01-restaurant-in-thailand-serves-human-meat/

The question here is about the extent of the human meat industry. Is this merely a thing done by a couple of mentally ill criminals or is there an actual widespread market, a Billion-Dollar industry around this? How common is it?

When researching conspiracies, the most pertinent question, often left unanswered, is about the *scope* of the conspiracy.

For instance, a local Catholic church had a "pedophile scandal". It was found that the priest had raped dozens of children inside the church building. Witnesses had come forward, his DNA had been sampled, he was arrested. The mainstream media treat these cases out-of-context, as if they were singular cases of derangement. But if you look closely–very closely–you'll find a "pedophile scandal" around Catholic Churches in every country, not just in your local area. The scope of it is global and much, much worse than most people are prepared to accept.

Nuns used crucifixes to rape girls during decades of abuse carried out by clergy in France's Catholic Church that saw attacks on 330,000 children covered up 'by a veil of silence', damning report finds

- Pope Francis expressed to the victims his 'great sorrow, for their wounds'
- An estimated 330,000 children were victims of sex abuse in France since 1950
- Scale of the number of attacks was covered up for decades by a 'veil of silence'
- Report was released Tuesday after after two-and-a-half-years of investigations

By CLARE MCCARTHY and PETER ALLEN FOR MAIL ONLINE and ASSOCIATED PRESS
PUBLISHED: 00:12 EDT, 5 October 2021 | UPDATED: 19:47 EDT, 5 October 2021

7.5k shares   **2.9k** View comments

https://www.dailymail.co.uk/news/article-10059827/Major-report-expose-sex-abuse-Frances-Catholic-Church.html

But because cases are viewed as single-incident, the Institution called "Catholic Church" can continue on as if nothing had happened. If people were aware of the scope of the problem, they'd have shut down the "Church" long ago. They'd realize that this Church has either been infiltrated by evil or was evil all along.

I realize there are Catholics among the readers of this book. I don't mean disrespect to your belief. Jesus Christ is most assuredly pro-human, anti-reptilian. But at the very least you need to look into what the top-tier of your organization are doing. Demand transparency.

And what is the scope of the human meat market? Now and then local news publishes an article of how some restaurant owner is arrested for stocking human meat in his refrigerator. These articles are usually local-news only, they don't make national headlines. People write it off as a freak-incident. Their attention span isn't high enough to realize that we have such headlines *every couple of weeks.*

The ultra-secretive human meat market gets exposed regularly because there are just too many people nosing around. But it's easy to wipe information off of the internet. By the time this book is published, some links shown here will probably no longer work. And stories like these will probably be "memory-holed":

FOX 29 WFLX.COM

☰ News Weather Hurricane Guide Traffic Sports Calendar South Florida Weekend Watch Live Savvy in 60 Conte

Dead body found inside Arby's restaurant freezer, police say

By Emily Van de Riet
Published: May. 12, 2023 at 12:42 PM EDT

The scope of the human meat market is so big in fact, that we have terms like "mystery meat" to describe meat of uncertain origin:

Mystery meat is a disparaging term for meat products that have an unidentifiable source, typically ground or otherwise processed foods such as

burger patties, chicken nuggets, Salisbury steaks, sausages and hot dogs. Most often the term is used in reference to food served in institutional cafeterias, such as prison food or a North American school lunch.

The term is also sometimes applied to meat products where the species from which the meat has come from is known, but the cuts of meat used are unknown. This is often the case where the cuts of meat used include offal and mechanically separated meat, or when non-meat substitutes such as textured vegetable protein are used to stretch the meat, where explicitly stating the type of meat used might diminish the perceived palatability of the product to some purchasers

https://en.wikipedia.org/wiki/Mystery_meat

Image: Lu Shaofei, Human Meat Market Shanghai (1929)

The image above is dated to the 1270s and can be found in the Getty Museum, Los Angeles. It is from the manuscript *Livre des Merveilles du Monde* (Marvels of the World). Depictions of casual cannibalism are common in medieval works, reports and even official documents (such as that of a 1000-person eating Cannibal by the name of Sawney Bean). Cannibalism has always been around.

Indigenous people around the world, including the native Americans, spoke of Giants eating humans. The Giants, according to the Bible, were the offspring of "fallen angels" forbidden sexual relations with humans. But there are also plenty of accounts and drawings of cannibalistic humans among the native Americans, as well as images of European and Spanish settlers and conquistadores having meat stalls where they offered and traded in human body parts.

There is also no shortage of medieval paintings in which demons and serpents are the flesh eaters, as in the painting below.

It was also normal to depict royalty as flesh-eaters, favouring baby-meat in particular. They were hated by the medieval "peasants" for this. The so-called "peasants" were simply human beings, whereas the "royalty" could very well have been reptilian in human disguise.

Examples of old news articles that relate to trade in human flesh:

TRADE IN *HUMAN* FLESH.
During the American war the British government *purchased the subjects of the German Princes*; now, the tables are turned, and the German Princes *purchase British subjects of the British government*. It is however of very little consequence who is the *buyer* or the *seller*—the *infamous trade* is still the same.

In case you can't read the printed image, this news-item from the early 1800s says: *Trade in Human Flesh during the American war the British government purchased the subjects of the German Princes: now, the tables are turned, and the German princes purchase British subjects of the British government. It is however of very little consequence who is the buyer or the seller—the infamous trade is still the same.*

ODDLY ENOUGH   NOVEMBER 16, 2009 / 3:08 PM / UPDATED 14 YEARS AGO

Cannibals nabbed selling corpse to kebab house

By Reuters Staff   1 MIN READ   f   𝕪

This news-item, also from the early 1800s says:

Prime Africans!!! Arrived at Charleston (S.C.) August 9-10, ship Aeriel Paine, from Africa, with 260 slaves and the British ship Esther, Erving, with a CARGO OF HUMAN FLESH, to the Charleston market—The whole consigned to Wm. Boyd!

Unlike today, the human meat market was practiced out in the open. News-items like these, start disappearing in the late 1800s, when the industry went underground, only to emerge every couple of weeks when another arrest occurs:

ODDLY ENOUGH   NOVEMBER 16, 2009 / 3:08 PM / UPDATED 14 YEARS AGO

Cannibals nabbed selling corpse to kebab house

By Reuters Staff   1 MIN READ   f   𝕪

Even though mainstream media is heavily redacted and censored, we still have an almost bi-weekly feed of horror stories that are mind-blowing in the negative sense. By now I've read at least a dozen stories where "grooming gangs" are somehow mixed in with the human meat industry. Why do pedophilia and cannibalism often arise together? Because these are things demonic entities like. They are two different types of energy-harvesting. Let me ask you again: What do you know about human harvesting?

Mum's anguish 15 years after her daughter was 'cut up and mixed into kebabs by grooming gang'

The mother of a missing schoolgirl feared murdered by grooming gangs has told how she will 'never stop fighting' for the truth.

Charlene Downes went missing 15 years ago this week - aged 14.

Her parents, Karen and Bob, were forced to endure courtroom claims her body was cut up and mixed into kebabs.

Now Charlene's mother has written an emotional book detailing the family's never-ending anguish as a warning to other parents.

Unable to have a funeral for her daughter, she holds memorials on every anniversary of her disappearance.

Source: https://www.manchestereveningnews.co.uk/news/greater-manchester-news/charlene-downes-blackpool-murder-kebabs-15343307

My Time Covering the Story of Charlene Downes, the Teenager 'Who Ended Up in a Kebab'

Ahead of a VICE Studios-produced documentary about the 2003 murder, journalist Joe Cusack - who has covered the story since it began - remembers his time on the beat.

JC By Joe Cusack

Source: https://www.vice.com/en/article/xwnaka/charlene-downes-murder-channel-5-vice

There is no other way to frame this stuff than utter disdain for humankind. Not only do they not mind exploiting children, they then go on to chop them up and feed them to the unsuspecting populace. I can't imagine a more hateful attitude.

The human meat conspiracy may seem like an obscure topic, but it keeps showing itself in "popular culture". That's because it's happening but suppressed to the collective subconscious.

There's the 1973 science-fiction movie "Soylent Green" with Charlton Heston. The populace eats a supposedly artificial substance called "Soylent Green". It later turns out that this is really human meat. Strangely enough, the movie is directed by Richard Fleischer. Fleisch is the German word for Meat and Fleischer an old German word for Butcher.

The 2010s film "Cloud Atlas" by the makers of "The Matrix" references humans as food for the Giants and the wealthy.

The 2010s TV Series Westworld does not directly reference human meat but comes close to it. It shows how elites exploit human beings for rape, fun and games.

The Chinese movie "Dumplings" shows how the wealthy prefer human meat for strength, beauty and youth.

"The Farm", a 2018 movie probably comes closest to showing what human farming and harvesting really is.

Movie critics write that the movie is a mere "allegory" on environmentalism, but that's not it at all. People are kept in cages and processed as meat to wealthy clients. I am, by the way, not recommending any of these movies. To me they all, at some level, promote the human farming agenda rather than warning of it and showing a way out. If you watch them and become disgusted, don't blame me, I'm just the messenger.

One of my favourite old movies "The Time Machine", 1959, written by intelligence operative H.G. Wells is about a subterranean group of creatures called Morlocks (a reference to Moloch) who are preying on humans called Eloi (a reference to Elohim), who thought they live in a kind of paradise but are really nothing more than food being grown and waiting to be eaten.

In 2013 Scarlett Johansson played in a movie titled "Under the Skin" which initially looks like it's about dissociative identity disorder or mkultra but finally turns out to be about aliens that process and consume the blood and flesh of human beings.

One our most famous fairy tales, Hansel and Gretel is about eating children. Consistent with that, many motifs of the middle-ages show children being eaten by dragons, giants and other creatures. There are in fact so many examples of the reptilian agenda in popular culture that one cannot really say "it doesn't exist". Even if it didn't exist as a tangible reality, it does exist as a fear in our psyche. And there is a reason for that fear. I'd go so far as to say that the reptilian agenda *is the most common theme* in fairy tales, legends and "mythology". Many tales ancient and modern are veiled allegories on the very same topic, many times over. So, while this book may seem highly unusual to you, it follows a very old tradition of anti-reptilian sentiment.

Human skin, fat, meat and blood have been used to create soap and leather products and many other things. Their bones and blood have been used as building material. Humans have been used as slaves and toys.

Wait, what…did I say our bones and blood are used to make buildings? Well, yes. None of what I am saying in this book is a secret. It's in the fine details, the small print. Our Overlords bank on the fact that we don't bother to look more closely because we are so "busy" with surviving. And even if we did look more closely, we wouldn't see it as what it is because most of us don't want to believe it's happening. And that's how these issues can stay "secret" even when happening in plain sight.

If you look up United States Patent 4203674 you find an item titled "Use of blood in the cement, mortar and concrete industry for obtaining a lightened material". The patent text further says:

"The present invention relates to the use of blood in the construction and building industry, whereby blood and extracts of blood containing haemoglobin are used as air entraining colloids. The recommended process for preparing a lightened material consists in association a construction element chosen from the cements, mortars and concretes, with at least one air entraining colloid chosen from whole blood, globules, red blood corpuscles and haemoglobin. The invention also relates to the lighted material obtained according to this process."

The reason a patent was granted on this, is because it's been practiced for much longer than people know. In the old days, the blood of sacrificed humans was mixed with the cement to "consecrate" a building according to arcane rituals.

From an article on CNBC:

Companies are making human-skin products to curb animal-testing of products

L'Oreal's EpiSkin is tempering the public outcry over animal testing that's plagued the cosmetics industry for decades.

MatTek's EpiDerm is EpiSkin's biggest competitor. The company produces about two adult humans' worth of skin every week.

Source: https://www.cnbc.com/2017/05/25/loreal-is-making-lab-produced-human-skin-to-curb-animal-testing.html

There is an entire Wikipedia page on Soap made from Human Corpses. I quote from that page:

"…Sigmund Mazur, a laboratory assistant at the Danzig Anatomical Institute, testified that soap had been made from corpse fat at the institute, and he also claimed that 70 to 80 kg (155–175 lb) of fat which was collected

from 40 bodies could produce more than 25 kg (55 lb) of soap, and the finished soap was retained by Professor Rudolf Spanner. Two British POWs who had to perform auxiliary tasks at the Institute provided witness-accounts.

Source: https://en.wikipedia.org/wiki/Soap_made_from_human_corpses

This is what is meant by human harvesting. The title of this book is called "What do you know about human harvesting?" I trust you now know something about it. But wait, there's more. From the same page:

In 1780, the former Holy Innocents' Cemetery in Paris was closed because of overuse. In 1786, the bodies were exhumed, and the bones were moved to the Catacombs. Many bodies had incompletely decomposed and had reduced into deposits of fat. During the exhumation, this fat was collected and subsequently turned into candles and soap.

There is a Wikipedia page "Lampshades made from Human Skin". There is another one about the binding of books with Human Skin. From this page I quote:

Anthropodermic bibliopegy is the practice of binding books in human skin. As of April 2022, The Anthropodermic Book Project has examined 31 out of 50 books in public institutions supposed to have anthropodermic bindings, of which 18 have been confirmed as human and 13 have been demonstrated to be animal leather instead.

Source: https://en.wikipedia.org/wiki/Anthropodermic_bibliopegy

I am not making the claim that all instances of human harvesting are nefarious. In some cases, skin, bone and blood are voluntarily donated. But the overall mentality behind human skin, flesh and blood industries is that of treating humans on par with animals.

From the Wikipedia page titled "Human Fat" (bolding mine)

Human fat was mentioned in European pharmacopoeias since the 16th century as an important fatty component of quality deemed ointments and other pharmaceuticals in Europe. In old recipes human adipose tissue was

111

mentioned as Pinguedo hominis, or Axungia hominis (abbrev. Axung. hominis), besides other animal fats from bears (Axung. ursi), vipers (Axung. viperarum), beavers (Axung. castoris), cats (Axung. Cati sylvestris) and many others. The German medicinal Johann Agricola (1496–1570) described the recovery of human fat and its applications.

*In traditional medicine in Europe, human fat was believed to have a **healing magic significance until the 19th century.** Many executioners recovered the fat from the bodies of their executants, called "Armsünderfett" or "Armsünderschmalz" (German for fat or grease from poor sinners put to death), and sold it. For some executioners the marketing of human fat was a major source of revenue. In traditional medicine many other parts of executed bodies as well as their fat were awarded a special action force, which evolved from a **pagan sacrificial belief.** The human fat was used to make ointments for treatment of various diseases such as bone pain, toothache and gout. It was also regarded as a panacea for particular diseases associated with cachexia (e.g. tuberculosis). Also an analgesic effect in rheumatoid arthritis was given to human fat.*

***Until the 1960s** various manufacturers offered alleged wrinkle creams for external use (Hormocenta of Hormocenta Cosmetic Böttger GmbH, or Placentubex C of Merz Pharmaceuticals) **containing human fat from placentas** collected from midwives and obstetric departments for industrial purposes*

Source: https://en.wikipedia.org/wiki/Human_fat

Did you know there are plenty of people who eat the human placenta? The practice is so common that hospitals and healthcare providers feature comments on it on their websites:

While some claim that placentophagy can prevent postpartum depression; reduce postpartum bleeding; improve mood, energy and milk supply; and provide important micronutrients, such as iron, there's no evidence that eating the placenta provides health benefits. Placentophagy can be harmful to you and your baby.

Mayo Clinic
https://www.mayoclinic.org › faq-20380880 ⋮

Eating the placenta: A good idea? - Mayo Clinic

Even though the intent here is probably not nefarious, eating the placenta is eating human meat. There's no other way to put it.

The following is from a BBC news article published on April 2, 2001. The context of this article is that the people of Moldova are poor, and that's why the state-run hospital resorts to letting people sell human meat. Is that so? Is this what humans do when they are poor? I'm aware of plenty of poor people who don't resort to such anti-human activities.

"Human meat traded in Moldova.

Authorities in Moldova have launched an investigation at a cancer clinic after two men were caught selling body parts as animal meat on the street.

The men told police that they got the parts—including a breast and legs—from the state clinic in Chisinau.

Moldova's average monthly salary is just $30

Police arrested them after a customer who bought meat at their makeshift stall outside a butcher's shop in the capital became suspicious.

Tests proved that the meat, which the men were selling for less than $2 a kilo, was human flesh. The men were arrested for selling meat without a licence.

The clinic, which is obliged to incinerate body parts, now faces penalties for not disposing of the parts in the correct way.

Ten years after gaining its independence, Moldova has been declared the poorest country in Europe.

The average monthly salary is just $30 and many of the 4.5 million inhabitants, especially in rural areas, are paid in crops and other goods.

Many people have not received a wage in months—if they have a job at all.

A series of droughts left farmers struggling to maintain production.

Organs for sale

And severe cold towards the end of 2000 ruined crops and downed tens of thousands of electricity pylons, bringing chaos to towns and villages in central and northern Moldova.

Unable to feed their families, Moldovans are prepared to go to extreme lengths to find better-paid work overseas, leaving many villages almost deserted.

In February, BBC News Online reported the plight of Moldovans who sell their body parts for cash after the World Health Organisation warned that the practice had become an industry in Moldova.

Many Moldovans sell their organs to so-called recruiters acting for agents in western Europe, Turkey and Israel.

Some donors are sent on to Georgia; other operations have been conducted in the Estonian capital, Tallinn.

We learn here that the practice is "an industry" in Moldova, but the beneficiaries are outside of the country. Israel, Turkey, Estonia and Western Europe can't be considered "poor".

It's true that crime organizations exploit the poor, knowing to what lengths they will go to provide for their families. Poverty benefits criminals. If you had the choice to let your family starve or commit a few crimes, you'd be hard pressed to resist the temptation.

If there is a clandestine human meat industry, what kind of infrastructure would support this? How could this possibly be happening outside of public knowledge? I say it's not that difficult because most people do not care or notice what numerous warehouses are used for, what shipping containers are used for, what tunnels and tunnel-systems are used for. There are tunnels under every city, tunnels below villages, tunnels connecting churches and chapels and tunnels connecting caves and the broad majority couldn't care less.

What if I told you there are secret tunnels and passages under *every* Church? Would you find that odd? Well, I'm telling you:

There's a tunnel under every Church.

It's a hidden infrastructure in every city, town and village used from ancient to modern times. You don't have to take my word for it, you can prove it yourself.

Typing "tunnel below church" into Google, generates 27 million results. How's that for proof?

These are only the results from half of the first page, I encourage you to read every headline and snippet:

About 27,900,000 results (0.53 seconds)

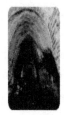

Live Science
https://www.livescience.com › Archaeology ⋮

Hidden tunnel and rooms unearthed under 1500-year-old ...

Jun 1, 2023 — Archaeologists excavating **beneath** the ruins of an early Christian **church** have unearthed underground rooms and a **tunnel** from 1,500 years ago in ...

The News & Observer
https://www.newsobserver.com › news › article238420983 ⋮

Mysterious tunnel discovered beneath VA Catholic church

Dec 16, 2019 — Crews took a closer look and discovered a **tunnel beneath** the Catholic **church** in downtown Norfolk, WVEC reports. Its existence ignites questions ...

▶ Videos ⋮

Tunnel found under historic Norfolk Church

YouTube · WAVY TV 10
Dec 4, 2019

3:39

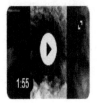

Tunnel discovered below Norfolk basilica

YouTube · 13News Now
Dec 17, 2019

1:55

Cool Finds

Archaeologists Discover Entrance to the Zapotec Underworld Beneath a Church in Mexico

New scans of the site have confirmed the existence of an "underground labyrinth"

Sonja Anderson

Reporter

July 18, 2023

HOME > DESIGN

1,500-Year-Old Underground Chambers, Tunnel Unearthed Beneath an Early Christian Church in Istanbul

Margaret Davis Jun 02, 2023 07:12 AM EDT

Seacoastonline.com

https://www.seacoastonline.com › local › 2021/08/07   ⋮

Basement tunnels lend mystery to St. John's history ...

Aug 7, 2021 — A **tunnel** which runs **underneath** the sanctuary of St. John's Episcopal **Church** in Portsmouth is. As recounted in a 2015 Seacoastonline article by ...

WAVY.com

https://www.wavy.com › news › local-news › tunnel-and...   ⋮

Tunnel and other historic artifacts found under Norfolk ...

Dec 4, 2019 — Mary of the Immaculate Conception discovered pieces of history when working at the **church**. They came across a **tunnel** and three crypts about two ...

WSBT

https://wsbt.com › news › local › secret-tunnels-under-...   ⋮

Secret tunnels under a South Bend church? Archaeology ...

Jun 22, 2016 — Secret **tunnels under** a South Bend **church**? Archaeology student digs into Studebaker past. by Danielle Kennedy, WSBT 22 Reporter. Wed, June 22nd ...

Liverpool Echo

https://www.liverpoolecho.co.uk › ... › Kirkby   ⋮

Legend behind the secret tunnels buried under a ...

Jan 2, 2021 — One resident said: "Most old **churches** have **tunnels beneath** them. It enabled priests, if no one else, to escape in troubled times." Another ...

Jerusalem Post

https://www.jpost.com › Israel News

Illegal church-built tunnel on Mount Zion concealed by ...

Mar 10, 2021 — There are many archaeological ruins buried **beneath** the area from the era of King David, the Hasmonean dynasty and the First **Temple**; a **tunnel** ...

 WordPress.com

https://lostinjersey.wordpress.com › 2009/03/06 › dutc...

Dutch Reformed Church and the tunnel under the Passaic ...

Mar 6, 2009 — The **church** is a historic building, but it's probably more well known for a **tunnel** that may or may not link the **church** to buildings on the other ...

 Utah Stories

https://utahstories.com › 2018/04 › what-lies-beneath-t...

What Lies Beneath? Tunnels under Salt Lake City

Apr 16, 2018 — **Underneath** the Mormon **Temple** in Downtown Salt Lake City, a series of **tunnels** spreads out in all directions. The earliest written mention of ...

Hürriyet Daily News

https://www.hurriyetdailynews.com › tunnel-that-leads... ⋮

Tunnel that leads to church found under house

Dec 23, 2020 — Security units have found a **tunnel**, which is some 30 meters deep and leads to a **church** nearby, **under** a house, which they raided in the Balat ...

 ashevilleoralhistoryproject.com

https://ashevilleoralhistoryproject.com › 2013/05/01 ⋮

The Ghost Sentry and the Secret Tunnel Under New Hope ...

May 1, 2013 — At the end of the day we found ourselves in the parking lot of the New Hope **Church**, site of a bloody Civil War battle in 1864. They had finished ...

 WBAL-TV

https://www.wbaltv.com › article › cumberland-churc... ⋮

Cumberland church served as hub for Underground ...

Feb 6, 2018 — David Hillhouse Buel, who was already active in the Underground Railroad in Maryland, felt the **tunnels underneath** the **church** would be a ...

TripAdvisor

https://www.tripadvisor.com › LocationPhotoDirectLi... ⋮

Picture of Real de Asientos Pueblo Magico

Real de Asientos Pueblo Magico, Asientos Picture: **Tunnel under church** of Asientos - Check out Tripadvisor members' 110 candid photos and videos of Real de ...

rameshchandramd.com
https://www.rameshchandramd.com › elbow-ramesh-g... ⋮

Cubital Tunnel Syndrome Treatment Falls Church, VA | Elbow ...

The lower arm or forearm consists of two bones, the radius and the ulna. Find out more about Normal Anatomy of the Elbow, click on **below** links. Patient Info ...

Atlas Obscura
https://www.atlasobscura.com › places › church-hill-tu... ⋮

Church Hill Tunnel – Richmond, Virginia

Oct 24, 2017 — Discover **Church Hill Tunnel** in Richmond, Virginia: **Under** a playground is a little-known sealed train **tunnel** that likely contains the bodies ...

Red Cliffs Desert Reserve
http://www.redcliffsdesertreserve.com › attachment ⋮

Tunnel Entrance Under I-15 - St. George

Tunnel under I-15 is a popular access for bikers leading directly to **Church** Rocks trail. Previous · Next · Explore the Reserve.

I've only screenshot a small sampling and we already know of tunnels below churches in Norfolk, Istanbul, Mexico, Portsmouth, South Bend, Salt Lake City, Liverpool, Jerusalem, another one in Turkey, Asheville, Asientos, and Maryland.

But I said there are tunnels under *every* Church. Surely I can't be serious? Shouldn't I be saying "some" or at the very best "many" Churches? But so far I've found a tunnel under *every* Church I've personally researched or inquired about, in different countries and on different continents.

Something is going on here that 99.9% of the public are not aware of. And it's going on right beneath our feet. What could it be?

I could Google "tunnel under Church" and then add a random country where Churches are common and would still get tens of thousands of results. Let me try right now.

Google   tunnel under church argentina   X ⊙ Q

Q All   🖼 Images   📰 News   ⊙ Maps   ▶ Videos   ⋮ More   Tools

About 24,300,000 results (0.45 seconds)

It was meant to be a secret. According to Schávelzon's research, the tunnels beneath the Manzana de las Luces were likely one part of a much larger (and unfinished) plan to connect the city's churches to allow priests and their congregations to escape in the event of an attack.

Jan 25, 2018

■■■ BBC
https://www.bbc.com › travel › article › 20180124-the-... ⋮

The mysterious tunnels beneath Buenos Aires - BBC Travel

                                          ❓ About featured snippets · 🚩 Feedback

Ⓐ Atlas Obscura
https://www.atlasobscura.com › places › manzana-de-l... ⋮

La Manzana de las Luces – Buenos Aires, Argentina

Mar 11, 2010 — Discover La Manzana de las Luces in Buenos Aires, **Argentina**: A gateway to a mysterious network of **underground tunnels**.

Google   tunnel under church estonia   X   ⊙   Q

Q All   🖻 Images   ⊙ Maps   🗐 News   ▶ Videos   ⋮ More   Tools

About 6,400,000 results (0.36 seconds)

    Sooloiluja
https://sooloiluja.com › Etusivu › Blog index ⋮

Bastion Passages: a long walk through the history

Apr 13, 2020 — Bastion passages: eye candy and history. From the lower end of the stairs
opens an impressive sight: endless looking vaulted **tunnel** illuminated ...

VT   Visit Tallinn
https://visittallinn.ee › see-do › attractions-museums ⋮

Bastion passages in the Tallinn Old Town

The mysterious passages **in** Tallinn's earthwork fortifications were built along with the
bastions **in** the 17th and 18th centuries to conceal the movement of ...

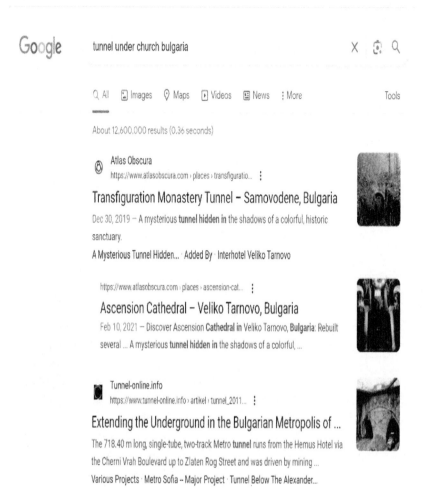

Three randomly chosen countries - Argentina, Estonia, Bulgaria. Same phenomenon: Tunnels under Churches!

But why? And how was it possible to keep this fact mostly secret? What is this infrastructure for?

Tunnels allow you to *operate* away from public view. If there are things you wish to do that, you don't want the public to see, tunnels are the best solution. Things you want the public to see, you do in the open. Tunnels have been used to smuggle goods, transport valuables, traffic drugs and weapons, abduct, kidnap and traffic humans and children. They have been used to convene secret meetings. Something you don't want the public to see is 9 times out of 10, nefarious.

Gruesome discoveries below Catholic Churches are common. Children's bodies have been found. Hundreds of thousands of Skulls have been found piled under Churches or even decoratively lining tunnels.

Shady people tend to hide behind good people. That's why Churches are susceptible to criminal activity. Churches are of course not the only buildings that have tunnels under them. You find tunnels under townhalls, castles, synagogues, mosques, temples, masonic lodges, casinos etc. but I'm singling out Churches because it's an institution people least suspect.

Here's just one (of thousands) of examples so that you get an idea of what tunnels are used for.

From the Wikipedia page titled Shanghai Tunnels:

*The **Old Portland Underground**, better known locally as the **Shanghai tunnels**, is a group of passages in Portland, Oregon, United States, mainly underneath the Old Town Chinatown neighborhood and connecting to the main business section. The tunnels connected the basements of many hotels and taverns to the waterfront of the Willamette River. They were built to move goods from the ships docked on the Willamette to the basement storage areas, allowing businesses to avoid streetcar and train traffic on the streets when delivering their goods.*

The newspapers of the 19th century document tunnels and secret passages underground. Organized crime was the center of many of these stories. However, many of the more colorful stories claimed for the underground are controversial. Historians have stated that although the tunnels exist and the practice of shanghaiing was sometimes practiced in Portland, as elsewhere, there is no evidence that the tunnels were used for this.

Source: https://en.wikipedia.org/wiki/Shanghai_tunnels

The word "Shanghaiing" means to kidnap people. It originates from rumors about people being kidnapped and taken through tunnels to serve as sailors or slave labor, something apparently common at one point in Shanghai.

Here's from the Wikipedia page on *Tunnels in popular culture:*

Mysterious tunnels or "secret passages" are a common element of the local folklore tradition in Europe. Such tunnels are said to physically link prominent places such as country houses, castles, churches, ancient monuments and other, often medieval, buildings.

Legends about the existence of secret tunnels usually involve improbably long subterranean passages, sometimes running under major obstacles such as rivers and lakes to reach their destinations. Religious buildings, monks and the landed gentry are particularly common elements in many tunnel stories.

It is unlikely that many of the recorded tunnels exist physically, for this is a characteristic of their very nature; their significance lies in the number of similar legends of tunnels that have arisen and in connection with the more esoteric notions of channels or paths of earth energy, and such

Source: https://en.wikipedia.org/wiki/Tunnels_in_popular_culture

In the last two paragraphs the editors of this article seem to downplay the importance of tunnels. "There is no evidence that tunnels were used for this" (kidnapping) and "It is unlikely that many of the recorded tunnels exist physically" are two outright lies. There is something uniquely creepy about Wikipedia. Why would one downplay the existence of tunnels used for crime? There is overwhelming evidence for tunnels used for kidnapping, throughout History.

The page goes on to contradict itself by sharing some marvelously creepy stories. One example:

In the city of Aalborg, a tunnel is said to have run from the convent under the fjord to another convent near Sundby. This tunnel had branches which ran to an old bridge, two churches and to the castle of Aalborghus. A student once tried to explore the tunnels with a long cord, a sword and a light. The broken cord was retrieved, but the student was never seen again.

There is also no shortage of fairy tales, legends, news reports, stats on child abduction, child disappearance, child trafficking and child predators. If it is true, that child meat is favoured by Reptilians it would explain all in one simple swoop. History is filled with accounts where parents were required to "sacrifice" their first-born child. Religious institutions and communist states have been known to seize children, supposedly for education or re-education, labour camps, as child soldiers and who knows what else. Orphanages and Child Care centres have been embroiled in scandal after scandal on child abuse, child murder and child disappearances as anyone who cares to research this grim topic can find out. Just a few examples, out of thousands:

The Kincora Boys' Home was a boys' home in Belfast, Northern Ireland that was the scene of serious organised child sexual abuse, causing a scandal and attempted cover-up in 1980, with allegations of state collusion. The Northern Ireland Historical Institutional Abuse Inquiry (HIA) began examining allegations relating to the Home on 31 May 2016, including claims that there was a paedophile ring at the home with links to the intelligence services. Northern Ireland Secretary Theresa Villiers said that all state agencies would co-operate with the inquiry.

Source: https://en.wikipedia.org/wiki/Kincora_Boys%27_Home

The Casa Pia child sexual abuse scandal was a case of child sexual abuses involving a number of children and employees at Casa Pia, a Portuguese state-run institution for the education and support of poor children and underage orphans. One employee of the institution, which at the time comprised 10 orphanages and schools caring for 4,600 children, ran a male child prostitution network involving 100 boys. The scandal involved several prominent men, including TV presenter Carlos Cruz, former Casa Pia governor Manuel Abrantes, and former UNESCO ambassador Jorge Ritto. The trial was one of the longest running in Portuguese history, lasting more than five years, with testimony from 32 alleged victims, out of a total of over 800 witnesses and experts.

Source: https://en.wikipedia.org/wiki/Casa_Pia_child_sexual_abuse_scandal

The Franklin child prostitution ring allegations took place between 1988 and 1991 and involved an alleged child sex ring serving prominent citizens of Nebraska, as well as high-level U.S. politicians. The allegations also claimed that the alleged sex ring was led by "a cult of devil worshipers involved in the mutilation, sacrifice and cannibalism of numerous children." The allegations centred on the actions of Lawrence E. King Jr., who ran the now defunct Franklin Community Federal Credit Union (FCFCU) in Omaha, Nebraska.

Source: https://infogalactic.com/info/Franklin_child_prostitution_ring_allegations

The Wall Street Journal reported in 2012 that: "It is estimated that some 8 million children go missing around the world each year". This is only the reported number.

I don't mean to sound racist, or better yet, specie-ist. But if there were only a human presence on this planet, would this many children go missing? Do you personally know any human being even remotely interested in abusing, molesting, raping or eating children? I have never met a single human being who would even entertain the thought. The propaganda tells us that "humans are just evil" and that's why millions of children go missing. But I don't believe that. It doesn't match my personal experience nor the experience of people I've listened to. I'm not denying that humans can turn evil and commit horrendous acts. I am denying that human's would commit these acts to such an extreme that 8 Million children go missing each year. 8 Million! That's eight cities put together. Are parents really this neglectful? Are predators really this common? I have my doubts.

Medieval paintings not only depict a lot of cannibalism, they also had the infrastructure to practice it openly. Perhaps it used to be done openly and became more underground over time. A typical feature of medieval butchers and halls were the long cooking spits—so long that they could cook "long pig" (a code word for humans). That gives a whole new meaning to the medieval term "burned at stake". Medieval times had a thriving "grave robbing" trade, involving the buying and selling of body parts. It seems that not all that much has changed since then:

Parts cut from donated bodies 'were sold illegally by staff at top US medical school'

Andrew Buncombe

But for who? Which *human being* would care to purchase the body parts of the dead? Again, I have personally met tens of thousands of people. I know many of them more intimately, from personal coaching. I have never come across anyone even remotely interested in purchasing the body parts of deceased humans. It's so far from normal human experience that it's not even a topic of discussion. When we learn it to be a Billion Dollar Industry and theme of thousands of shocker-news items, we begin to accept that our "elites" are very different from everyday people.

Another way "someone" gets a hold of humans is through purchasing or "leasing" convicts, criminals and even people who had been sentenced to death.

Penal labour in the United States is explicitly allowed by the 13th Amendment of the U.S. Constitution: "Neither slavery nor involuntary servitude, except as a punishment for crime whereof the party shall have been duly convicted, shall exist within the United States, or any place subject to their jurisdiction."

https://en.wikipedia.org/wiki/Penal_labor_in_the_United_States

Indentured servitude is a labour contract where an individual will work to repay an indenture or loan over some time, commonly several years. Indentured servitude was popular in American colonies as many worked in exchange for the price of passage to America.

https://www.investopedia.com/terms/i/indentured-servitude.asp

As far as I can tell, the law hasn't changed since then. It's still legal, in the U.S. to enslave people convicted of a crime.

With this kind of loophole, you understand stories about "elites" recruiting their henchmen and stooges among the inhabitants of prisons. "I'll pay for your bail and give you a second chance at life. But you work for me only". Most prisoners would choose slavery to sitting in an empty cell all day.

"FBI finds bodies sewn together 'like Frankenstein' in human chop shop.

Buckets of body parts, a cooler filled with male genitalia and a woman's head sewn onto a male torso "like Frankenstein" were found by FBI agents during a raid on an Arizona body donation center, a new lawsuit reveals.

The stomach-churning scene was discovered by FBI agents at the now-shuttered Biological Resource Center in 2014 as part of a multi-state investigation into the illegal trafficking and sale of human body parts, as reported by the Arizona Republic.

Details of the grim find were revealed in a lawsuit filed against the center this week by 33 plaintiffs whose loved ones' bodies were donated to the facility under the guise they would be used for scientific purposes.

In his declaration in the civil suit, former FBI special agent Mark Cwynar described the "various unsettling scenes" that awaited cops, including "a bucket of heads, arms and legs" and "a cooler filled with male genitalia."

Agents also found "infected heads," a small woman's head sewn onto a large male torso and hanging on a wall "like Frankenstein," and body parts stacked on top of one another with no identification tags.

Biological Resource Center specialized in the free pickup of deceased loved ones for families in exchange for their bodies, to be used for scientific research.

Instead, the company sold body parts to various middlemen for profit.

A 2013 price list included in the civil court filing indicates a whole boy with no shoulders or head could be purchased for $2,900 while a whole spine retailed for $950.

https://nypost.com/2019/07/25/fbi-finds-bodies-sewn-together-like-frankenstein-in-human-chop-shop/

I quoted the above article in full to drive home the point of human harvesting. There are entire books written on the illicit human body parts industry. According to the mainstream books on this, these criminal activities are conducted for "science" and "anatomy projects". But again, I have my doubts. If a body is needed for anatomy projects, there's no need to do it in secret.

There have been many cases in which funeral home owners are arrested for selling body parts to "scientists". It's said to be a "Billion Dollar Industry". Relatives of deceased people have been asked whether the bodies of their relatives could be used for "scientific research". Signing such a waiver apparently gives funeral homes the license to reuse and resell the cadaver. But many have also been found to sell body parts without such a waiver because the broad majority of people are not interested in exhuming the body once it's buried.

An example:

Funeral home operators sentenced after illegally selling body parts

Two funeral home operators in Colorado were sentenced Wednesday for illegally selling bodies and body parts without the families' consent, the US Attorney's Office said.

Megan Hess was sentenced to 20 years in prison and her mother, Shirley Koch, received 15 years for their involvement in the scheme to sell the human remains to body broker services, according to federal prosecutors. They each pleaded guilty to one count of mail fraud and aiding and abetting.

"These two women preyed on vulnerable victims who turned to them in a time of grief and sadness. But instead of offering guidance, these greedy women betrayed the trust of hundreds of victims and mutilated their loved ones," Leonard Carollo, the acting special agent in charge at the FBI in Denver, said in a news release.

"Without knowledge or consent, the women disrespected the wishes of the grieving victims and degraded the bodies of their family members to sell them for profit," Carollo said.

The women ran Sunset Mesa Funeral Home in Montrose, Colorado. From 2010 through 2018, they would meet with people seeking cremation services either for themselves or their loved ones, according to the plea agreement.

"In many instances, Koch and Hess neither discussed nor obtained authorization for donation of decedents' bodies or body parts for body broker services," the news release said.

Source: https://www.cnn.com/2023/01/04/us/colorado-funeral-home-body-parts/index.html

And so I ask you again: What do you know about human harvesting? Quite a lot by now! An idea that probably at first seemed vague when you first read the title of this book, comes sharply into focus. There are certain professions that are especially vulnerable to infiltration by anti-human agendas, such as daycare centers and funeral homes.

But how widespread is it all? What is the scope of this evil amongst us? Here's a headline to consider:

More than 225 thousand umbilical cord blood samples cryopreserved in a failed Swiss stem cell bank are missing.

Source: https://bioinst.com/en/swiss-umbilical-cord-blood-stem-cell-bank-failed-a-disaster-waiting-to-happen/

We've heard it said that reptilians rely on human flesh to maintain their human appearance. I don't know if this is true. It is true that flesh eating and blood drinking makes reptilians feel "high" for some time, similar to when we take drugs. In my book "Clearing Entities" I spoke of rituals of the Australian Aborigines which involved eating the flesh of a deceased person to catch "glimpses of heaven". It was believed that after a person died, their spirit was still connected to the body for some time and by ingesting their flesh, one could experience what they were seeing and feeling. Apparently, this is one of the primary purposes of cannibalism–having the life force to view or penetrate higher realms, even if only temporarily. An illegal way to ascend. It is for this reason, they say, that eating human flesh is highly addictive.

British royalty dined on human flesh (but don't worry it was 300 years ago)

By FIONA MACRAE FOR THE DAILY MAIL
UPDATED: 10:40 EDT, 6 March 2016

●**87**
View comments

They have long been famed for their love of lavish banquets and rich recipes. But what is less well known is that the British royals also had a taste for human flesh.

A new book on medicinal cannibalism has revealed that possibly as recently as the end of the 18th century British royalty swallowed parts of the human body.

The author adds that this was not a practice reserved for monarchs but was widespread among the well-to-do in Europe.

https://www.dailymail.co.ukl/news/article-1389142/British-royalty-dined-human-flesh-dont-worry-300-years-ago.html

I'm curious about the utter lack of curiosity on part of the journalists who write these stories. If royals used to do it, because it made them feel high and was viewed as extremely nutritious what's stopping them from doing it now? It is not mentioned when the practice was stopped, why it was stopped or who decided it would be stopped. For all we know, it could still be happening. The impression I get from much of this "journalism" is that it is sought out for shock-value, as clickbait. The stories are true, but there is no curiosity about their background or context. They are used to generate and hold attention on a website. There is no comparison to similar stories and no questioning of how such circumstances developed. News-media, itself governed by a reptilian-agenda, seems to care more about shock and awe than meta-research.

There are news stories so horrible I don't even want to share them here in this book full of already awful things. Yes, much more horrible than what's already shown. Things about what happens to aborted fetuses and who purchases fresh cadavers straight from hospitals. Stories of missing homeless people. And more.

So, I'll ask a softer question: Why won't food companies tell us where their meat comes from?

11 Food Companies That Won't Tell You Where Their Meat Comes From

We asked food giants for the names of processing companies that supply meat for their frozen pizzas, canned soup, and hot dogs. Only 2 out of 13 would share the info — even confidentially.

Source: https://www.buzzfeed.com/deenashanker/companies-that-wont-tell-you-about-their-meat

The problem with this list is that it encompasses most of the companies that sell food in our supermarket aisles. So, the next question is: Why are so many people eating food that cannot be traced to a source? I'm not being hypocritical here, because I myself always make sure I look into where my food comes from and I quit eating canned and processed food more than 20 years ago. If a company can't tell me where its foods are derived, I'm not interested in eating their food. Simple as that. Something that should arouse suspicion in every sentient being is simply ignored.

You see that "the reptilian agenda" is not only about reptilians, it is about the "reptilian" within ourselves, the apathetic, docile, uninterested, uninspired, listless self that won't ask the most basic questions about their daily life and reality.

Cartel cannibals! Mexican drug lords force new members to kill rivals and eat their HEARTS

- The Jalisco New Generation Cartel is making new recruits eat human flesh
- It shares videos of members eating rival gangs' hearts as a form of intimidation
- New cartel members start by eating toes before moving to bigger body parts

By JOE DAVIES FOR MAILONLINE
PUBLISHED: 09:03 EDT, 14 February 2022 | UPDATED: 12:28 EDT, 14 February 2022

I'm not interspersing this book with these articles for shock value but so that you gain an understanding of a completely different agenda and consciousness level. The drug cartel are not some random poor people, they are multi-billion-dollar global Businesses.

When a U.S. President says he wants to crackdown on the cartels or even send military after them, the press condemns the statements in unison as harsh, hardline or even "racist". But honestly, the cartels engage in cannibalism, child trafficking, child abuse, murder, political assassination, blackmail, intimidation and more. A mainstream media that defends such people is an anti-human media. Meanwhile, humans are too docile and intimidated to speak up. Here, I'll speak up: I fully support military action against the cartels. But there's another reason they still haven't been defeated. They are supported by our very own CIA. El Chapo Guzman is known to have cooperated with the CIA. CIA airplanes have often been found to traffic drugs for the cartel. If the existence of these anti-human criminals weren't in the interest of our government, they wouldn't exist anymore.

Here's a small snippet from a BBC article (bolding mine):

'Human meat' alert at pig farm

*Officials in western Canada have warned that **meat from a pig** farm owned by an accused serial killer may have been contaminated with **human remains**.*

British Columbia health officials issued an alert urging anyone who may have meat from Robert Pickton's farm near Vancouver to contact police.

*Mr Pickton, 54, has been charged with 15 murders of women, most of whom were linked to Vancouver's **sex trade**.*

Police say they have found the remains of more than 20 women at the farm.

Source: http://news.bbc.co.uk/1/hi/world/americas/3500890.stm

And here's a shocker of a news article, published in the Italian newspaper La Stampa on the 19th of September 2019.

Stem cells in Swiss biobank missing, a haven for 15,000 Italian mothers

A federal investigation has been launched to find out where the umbilical cord blood entrusted to Cryo-Save went.

A repository of umbilical cord blood samples at Cyro-Save, Europe's largest cord blood bank, mysteriously disappeared from their Geneva branch. The stem cell deposits went missing at the end of August and it's still a mystery how and where they've ended up. The Swiss judicial authority has opened an official investigation to look into the matter. Authorities are not just looking to track down where the samples went, but also how they were moved and how they had been stored for the last few years. These same questions are also being asked by the 15,000 Italian mothers who entrusted their children's cord blood to Cryo-Save.

Official complaints and searches

The federal prosecutor's office and the Office of Public Health launched their official investigation into the mysterious incident at the beginning of September. Fedpol conducted various searches last week, and initial reports issued by Swissmedic -the surveillance authority for medicines and medical devices- revealed signs of the company having committed several crimes, first and foremost by violating the law on transplants, which include a breach of contractual obligations regarding notification and cooperation. To complicate matters even further, the company operates in 30 different countries: Cryo-Save is a Swiss company listed in the Netherlands with a subsidiary in Italy...

Source: https://www.lastampa.it/esteri/la-stampa-in-english/2019/09/18/ news/stem-cells-in-swiss-biobank-missing-a-haven-for-15-000-italian-mothers-1.37482902/

I'm letting the reports speak for themselves. These are not my personal words or theories; they are crimes committed in the world you live in.

I'm not telling you all of this as a rant, I have actually been doing something about it and continue to work a pro-human agenda, as you'll learn in the last chapter.

Anyone who cares to look, will find "rumors" of mass human meat production for public consumption anywhere around the world. An example. Below is the cover for a book titled *"The Human Sausage Factory—A Study of a Postwar rumor in Tartu"*.

The book is a scholarly work that tries to "understand" why thousands of witnesses in the Estonian city of Tartu, would "make up rumors" for so many years. A simple answer to that is because they are not rumors. What's more likely, that thousands of people would risk their reputation for a fake story or that something nefarious was really happening? A few excerpts:

People were afraid to go there. For years there had been rumours about how the ruins of a sausage factory on Turu Street were burnt down. Strange women lured the plumper children there by giving them three roubles and asking them to deliver a letter to a particular place, where the child was made into sausages. Someone who had been lucky enough to escape this fate had seen with her own eyes headless human bodies hanging from the ceiling and blood dripping into a tin bowl, drip, drip, drip.

...

of things that should long ago have become part of a dim and distant past. This is what happened to many people living in the Estonian town of Tartu at the end of 2001. While systematising materials sent to the Estonian Folklore Archives I had noticed several texts recounting the story of a post-war "human sausage factory" in Tartu. Many texts refer to more or less the same location, which the war had reduced to ruins. That same autumn I gave an interview to a newspaper, Tartu Postimees, and when discussing urban folklore, referred to these texts as clear horror stories. As a response to this choice of words, an elderly man called the newspaper's editorial office, claiming that it was not folklore since his father had seen it all; allegedly he had been one of the many people who had witnessed it at that time. After the war, one day in perhaps 1947, when the caller's father was at Tartu market, a wounded and shocked woman ran into the marketplace screaming that people were being killed. The woman pointed to a site a few hundred metres from the marketplace. Dozens of people, including the informant's father, rushed to the ruins and entered through a burnt out gate patched with tin roofing and barbed wire. In the ruins the informant's father had seen human body parts, hair, piles of clothes and school notebooks. The wounded and disconcerted woman, a milkmaid, told the people from the marketplace how she had been approached by a Russian man who had asked her to sell milk to his friends a little way away, in the ruins. The milkmaid had gone there and when entering through the gate saw people unloading a corpse from a lorry. The woman was turning to run when someone threw an axe at her back. Scared and screaming, the woman had then returned to the marketplace. By the time the people arrived at the ruins with the wounded woman, the men had disappeared. Soon afterwards, the police surrounded the site.

This so-called rumor was spread among the populace in 1947 but it was quelled because the Soviet-Communist KGB was arresting anyone reporting the story.

Among the stories that were told during this period, there were rumours about sausage factories in several other Estonian cities then also in rack and ruin –Narva, Viljandi, Rakvere and Tallinn. For comparison, the same rumours also circulated in Latvia, Russia and elsewhere in Europe. The German narrative scholar Rolf Wilhelm Brednich has come upon written testimonies of an analogous story about Berlin in post-war literature and journalism.

In 1946 a young woman is walking along a street in Berlin and when passing the ruins, she suddenly stumbles upon a man who appears to be blind. Poking with his stick, the man galumphs through the rubble. The man names the place where he is supposed to go. The place is far away. The blind man asks if the woman would help him and at least take his letter to the destination. The woman agrees and, looking back, sees the man disappearing around the corner with an unusually fast and steady walk for a blind man. The woman takes the unopened letter to the police. The policemen arrest two men and a woman from the said address and find there a huge amount of meat which had the value of gold at the time. Then follows the shock: further investigation reveals that it is human flesh. The letter read: 'This is my last delivery today'

…

References to rumours about sausages made of human flesh can be found in a number of memoirs and diaries of the period.

…

This is the only such story I will quote, to keep the gore at a reasonable limit, without omitting what is going on.

This is from the annual register of London of the year 1801:

> 26th. About eight in the evening a mob assembled before a house in Wych Street, formerly the Queen of Bohemia tavern, (but now supposed to be unoccupied,) in consequence of some boys, who had been at play in the passage, declaring they saw some persons through the key hole employed in cutting up human bodies. The mob, having increased, at length broke into the house, in which they found several human bodies partly dissected, one body of a man which appeared to have been not long dead, with that of an infant not four months old, untouched, and several tubs with human flesh, &c. The stench was so great, that many were glad to return without viewing the disgusting scene, and many who went in were seized with sickness.

Normal human beings are "seized with sickness" regarding human flesh, blood, intestines and body parts. People engaged in this kind of practice–are they really "people"?

People say we are overpopulated, but if I look at it from a farming and harvesting perspective, we are crowded into cities like farm animals. When humans are more spread out, they usually live a more luxurious and dignified life. The crowding, surveilling, testing, injecting and constant influencing of humans is part of the anti-human agenda. If you truly love humankind, you're not interested in any of that.

Human Excrement as Fertilizer

Did you know that the ruling elite gets human beings to eat their own feces? I've shared this fact with some friends and none of them believed me. I couldn't be bothered to prove it to them, firstly because it's hard to find blatant evidence for covered-up crimes and secondly because it's not my job to disturb their sense of comfort.

But just because you don't know about it, doesn't mean it's not true. Type "sewage as fertilizer" into a search engine and you get hundreds of thousands of results. There are countless companies that specialize in this. For example, check the brandname "milorganite" on Wikipedia and you get this:

Milorganite is a brand of biosolids fertilizer produced by treating sewage sludge...The material is then pelletized and marketed throughout the United States under the name Milorganite. The result is recycling of the nitrogen and phosphorus from the waste-stream as fertilizer.

When you look up the term "Biosolids" on Wikipedia, you get this:

Biosolids are solid organic matter recovered from a sewage treatment process and used as fertilizer. In the past, it was common for farmers to use animal manure to improve their soil fertility. In the 1920s, the farming community began also to use sewage sludge from local wastewater treatment plants. Scientific research over many years has confirmed that these biosolids contain similar nutrients to those in animal manures. Biosolids that are used as fertilizer in farming are usually treated to help to prevent disease-causing pathogens from spreading to the public.

An interesting newspaper article from the Bristol Cable, titled "The Avonmouth explosion was horrific. But it wasn't unprecedented".

I quote from the article:

The business of recycling sewage into fertiliser, and the wider wastewater treatment industry, have been chequered by explosions and industrial accidents

...

Yet the huge blast at a Wessex Water waste treatment plant in Avonmouth followed a number of explosions, spillages and major incidents at similar facilities operated by other companies, in recent years.

The dirty business of recycling waste, which inevitably entails producing and storing flammable gases, doesn't come without risk. Plants are designed to prevent explosions, over-pressurisation, asphyxiation and pollution, but accidents do happen. At some sites, storage tanks with steel and concrete roofs have been known to rupture and even blast off, in scenes similar to that in Avonmouth.

...

'treated sludge' is transferred to storage silos before being sold to farmers.

https://thebristolcable.org/2021/02/the-avonmouth-explosion-was-horrific-but-it-wasnt-unprecedented-wessex-water-silo-bristol/

Yes, you read correctly—"wastewater and sludge" (your urine and excrement) is "treated" and then sold back to farmers who make your next food with it. That's the cycle of life, I guess. But as you see from the article, your excrement also has explosive qualities and can be used for many other purposes.

From an agricultural articled titled "Human Waste, not Want":

Human solid waste can be safely processed in various ways. Feces are a source of organic matter that can improve soil texture and its ability to absorb rainwater, mitigating the effects of drought on crop production.

Wastewater treatment plants turn solid wastes into "biosolids," which are regulated by the Environmental Protection Agency. Solid wastes, either biosolids or source-separated feces, can also be turned into biochar. This also can be added to the soil as a source of carbon.

Waste re-use in action

A few US cities have started using the biosolids from their wastewater systems. Tacoma, Washington, sells their biosolids under the name Tagro. Chicago, Illinois, is using biosolids in their urban remediation projects. The Rich Earth Institute, in Vermont, has a community pee-cycling program and has published a guide entitled "Guide to Starting a Community-scale Urine Diversion Program."

Eating human feces is arguably "cannibalism lite".

Some readers might wonder what the big deal is. There are philosophers, scientists and celebrities who openly advocate for cannibalism, as a protein-rich diet. They defend "ethical" consensus-based cannibalism. Famous atheist Richard Dawkins has recommended Cannibalism on several occasions. I once coached a student who runs one of the largest fitness-chains. He also advocated for ethical cannibalism, saying it's the "most fitness-conscious" diet. My skepticism, he said, is due to my religious conditioning.

If we believe the Abrahamic religions but also the traditions of the far-east (Buddhism, Taoism, Hinduism), humans were not made for consumption by our Creator. The only way you'd find Cannibalism OK, in my view, is if you're dulled to a point where you no longer believe in a Creator and a set of rules for life on Earth. Cannibalism is a defiance of the natural order.

You might argue that there are animals who cannibalize each other. People who equate animals and humans can't tell that these are two entirely different levels of consciousness. The ancients said that low-consciousness creatures are made for consumption. Doing so contributes to the natural cycle of life. Vegetarians disagree and consider eating animals a crime. But even animals eat animals. Are they committing a crime? Eating humans, I assert, goes against the higher order, turning humans into beasts. If you don't believe that cannibalism is bad, look what it does to the people who practice it and some of the other stuff they do. "If you're into this kind of stuff, you might also be interested in that stuff".

At the very least, everyone should know the context of cannibalism, which is not limited to "mentally deranged poor people" but practiced by billion-dollar-crime organizations, occultists and "elites". People should know the nature of "elites" and the scope of their crimes, which are far greater than generally assumed.

Image: Reptilian-humanoid figure of ancient Mesopotamia

7

Human Hunting

For centuries we've heard rumours of human hunting. We've read stories about how "the elites" have their private hunting grounds and send out humans to be hunted down for sport to be shot, raped or even eaten. Is such dehumanizing activity really taking place? If yes, we must put a stop to it. If not, we need to expose the liars claiming it does. There are no two ways about it. If true, it's harmful to society and we are the keepers of our brothers and sisters. And if not true, it's also harmful to society because it creates suspicion and apathy around our ability to run and protect our brothers and sisters.

Fiction is sometimes used to introduce truths to society without breaking non-disclosure agreements. I'll briefly go over a few fictional works on human hunting.

The Most Dangerous Game

"The Most Dangerous Game", also published as "The Hounds of Zaroff", is a short story by Richard Connell. first published in Collier's on January 19, 1924, with illustrations by Wilmot Emerton Heitland. The story features a

big-game hunter from New York City who falls from a yacht and swims to what seems to be an abandoned and isolated island in the Caribbean, where he is hunted by a Russian aristocrat...

The story has been adapted numerous times, most notably as the 1932 RKO Pictures film The Most Dangerous Game, starring Joel McCrea, Leslie Banks and Fay Wray,[6] and for a 1943 episode of the CBS Radio series Suspense, starring Orson Welles. It has been called the "most popular short story ever written in English."

Source: https://en.wikipedia.org/wiki/The_Most_Dangerous_Game

Hard Target

Hard Target is a 1993 American action film directed by Hong Kong film director John Woo in his U.S. debut. The film stars Jean-Claude Van Damme as Chance Boudreaux, an out-of-work homeless Cajun merchant seaman and former United States Force Recon Marine who saves a young woman named Natasha Binder (Yancy Butler) from a gang of thugs in New Orleans. Chance learns that Binder is searching for her missing father (Chuck Pfarrer), and agrees to aid Binder in her search. They soon learn that Binder's father has died at the hands of hunt organisers Emil Fouchon (Lance Henriksen) and Pik van Cleef (Arnold Vosloo), a ruthless businessman and his right-hand mercenary, who arrange the hunting of homeless men as a form of recreational sport.

Source: https://en.wikipedia.org/wiki/Hard_Target

Hostel (2005)

Paxton and Josh spend their summer after graduating college traveling the various countries in Europe. Exploring all manner of debaucherous activities, they befriend an Icelandic tourist named Óli. One night the trio are locked out of their hotel, and visit an apartment of a local named Alexei. After being told of a hostel run by seductive women in Slovakia, the friends make the journey to the rumoured location. Upon arrival they are pleased to find that Alexei's story was true, a location overrun by nude foreign women.

As they engage in various sexual encounters, over time they soon begin to question the intentions of the establishment. As Óli goes missing, the friends attempt to investigate his disappearance. When they are drugged by a pair of women that they had been associating in a sex-based relationship, they individually awaken to a horrific underground torture event, lead by a secret organization. The company allows wealthy individuals to pay large amounts of money to torture, maim, and kill abducted innocent tourists. Unwittingly finding themselves a part of the cult's activities, Paxton and Josh must fight for survival in the nightmare they've awoken in, or die by a series of gory events.

There are other movies with the same theme. "Race with the Devil" (1975), "Surviving the Game" and "The Naked Prey (1965) just to name a few. And there are hundreds of movies depicting elites playing games with and victimizing innocents. Again, if there is no reality to any of this, why is "popular culture" so full of it?

And then there are claimed non-fiction accounts. This is from the 1995 book *Trance-formation of America* by MKUltra abuse survivor Cathy O'Brien. O'Brien says that Dick Cheney, the 46th Vice President of the United States, enjoys human hunting.

In the summer of 1975, my family drove all the way from Michigan to the Teton Mountains of Wyoming. I was ordered to ride in the back storage area of the family Chevy Suburban since I was forbidden to associate or communicate with my brothers and sister. So, I dissociated into books, or into the metaphorical, hypnotic suggestions from my father and tranced deeper as I watched the prairie's seemingly endless sea of "amber waves of grain" streak past my window. Once when we stopped at a gas station, my father took me inside to show me a stuffed "jackalope" mounted on the wall. Due to my tranced, dissociative state and high suggestibility level, I believed it was indeed a cross between a jack rabbit and antelope. It was 100+ degrees in the Badlands when it cooled down at night. The intense heat of the day accentuated my ever-increasing thirst. My father was physically preparing me though water deprivation for the intense tortures and programming I would endure in Wyoming.

Dick Cheney, then White House Chief of Staff to President Ford, later Secretary of Defense to President George Bush, documented member of the Council on Foreign relations (CFR), and Presidential hopeful for 1996, was originally Wyoming's only Congressman. Dick Cheney was the reason my family had traveled to Wyoming where I endured yet another form of brutality — his version of "A Most Dangerous Game," or human hunting.

It is my understanding now that A Most Dangerous Game was devised to condition military personnel in survival and combat maneuvers. Yet it was used on me and other slaves known to me as a means of further conditioning the mind to the realization there was "no place to hide,"

as well as traumatize the victim for ensuing programming. It was my experience over the years that A Most Dangerous Game had numerous variations on the primary theme of being stripped naked and turned loose in the wilderness while being hunted by men and dogs. In reality, all "wilderness" areas were enclosed in secure military fencing whereby it was only a matter of time until I was caught, repeatedly raped, and tortured.

Dick Cheney had an apparent addiction to the "thrill of the sport." He appeared obsessed with playing A Most Dangerous Game as a means of traumatizing mind control victims, as well as to satisfy his own perverse sexual kinks. My introduction to the game occurred upon arrival at the hunting lodge near Greybull, Wyoming, and it physically and psychologically devastated me. I was sufficiently traumatized for Cheney's programming, as I stood naked in his hunting lodge office after being hunted down and caught. Cheney was talking as he paced around me, "I could stuff you and mount you like a jackalope and call you a two legged dear. Or I could stuff you with this (he unzipped his pants to reveal his oversized penis) right down your throat, and then mount you. Which do you prefer?"

Blood and sweat became mixed with the dirt on my body and slid like mud down my legs and shoulder. I throbbed with exhaustion and pain as I stood unable to think to answer such a question. "Make up your mind," Cheney coaxed. Unable to speak, I remained silent. "You don't

get a choice, anyway. I make up your mind for you. That's why you're here. For me to make you a mind, and make you mine/mind. You lost your mind a long time ago. Now I'm going to give you one. Just like the Wizard (of Oz) gave Scarecrow a brain, the Yellow Brick Road led you

here to me. You've 'come such a long, long way' for your brain, and I will give you one."

The blood reached my shoes and caught my attention. Had I been further along in my programming, I perhaps would never have noticed such a thing or had the capability to think to wipe it away. But so far, I had only been to MacDill and Disney World for government/military

programming. At last, when I could speak, I begged, "If you don't mind, can I please use your bathroom?"

Cheney's face turned red with rage. He was on me in an instant, slamming my back into the wall with one arm across my chest and his hand on my throat, choking me while applying pressure to the carotid artery in my neck with his thumb. His eyes bulged and he spit as he growled, "If you don't mind me, I will kill you. I could kill you —Kill you — with my bare hands. You're not the first and you won't be the last. I'll kill you any time I goddamn well please." He flung me on the cot-type bed that was behind me. There he finished taking his rage out on me sexually.

On the long trip back to Michigan, I lay in a heap behind the seats of the Suburban, nauseated and hurting from Cheney's brutality and high voltage tortures, plus the whole Wyoming experience. My father stopped by the waterfalls flowing through the Tetons to "wash my brain" of the memory of Cheney. I could barely walk through the woods to the falls for the process as instructed, despite having learned my lessons well from Cheney on following orders.

I was a young man in my early 20s when I read O'Brien's book, but apart from a sensationalistic thrill, it didn't mean anything to me. The idea of our trusted politicians and authorities engaging in psychopathic, criminally insane "leisure activities" didn't register in my mind until much later.

"Authoritative sources" assured us that O'Brien must be mentally ill to make such claims, and I mostly believed them. Mainstream has always insinuated that anyone who believes such things, must be mentally ill. Being a man in my 20s seeking a successful career, I certainly didn't wish to be grouped with the psychiatric nutjobs so I dismissed this book and others like it. Then why did I read it in the first place? Now I believe it was my higher-self, my intuitive-self choosing the books. My world-self laughed them off.

Once again so much happened and was revealed on the world stage about our "elites" that made me regret dismissing O'Brien's account. She was the very first widely read author to say that Bill and Hillary Clinton were sex-crazed rapists. That was completely contrary to their public image in the 90s. But after 2016, many people came to agree.

A few years after O'Brien published, the Lewinsky affair cast its first shadow on the sex life of the Clinton's. Then, in 2015, twenty years later, Wikileaks Julian Assange revealed Hillary Clinton as a person performing ritual sacrifice to Moloch. After that, an avalanche of information about the strange activities of the Clinton's came to public awareness. During those days I kept thinking back on O'Brien's book that had foreshadowed all these truths long before.

Two of the main premises of the 1995 book–the evils of the Bush family and the Clinton family, became apparent to most sentient beings in the decades that followed. If Trance-formation of America says that Human Hunting is "a thing", much like sport, among the "elites", then it's probably true.

There are also accounts of human hunting documented in courts of law. The 1996 Dutroux affair is the best example. The incident provided a rare insight into the pedophilia, child abuse, torture and utter disdain for human life by "elites". Marc Dutroux was arrested for kidnapping, torturing and raping six girls between ages 8 and 19, four of who died. Dutroux was subsequently shown to have trafficked children for sex to policemen, politicians and celebrities in Belgium. There was a widely publicized trial in 2004. It turns out that Dutroux and his friends organized hunting parties on naked and terrified children. Several girls and witnesses spoke about snuff films in which children were murdered and raped to death. Child-hunting parties often took place at the woods of the Chateau de Chamay, in the presence of various royalty that were named by name in the court dossiers. The Dutroux affair should have gotten people to look into the leisure activities of royal families and politicians in other countries, but it didn't happen. The case was filed away as a "single incident", once again. It astonishes me how, even when a court of law finds the involved parties guilty, any royal family members somehow get a pass.

This happened again, quite recently, when Prince Andrew was discovered to have been involved with Jeffrey Epstein's pedophile sex trafficking ring but got nothing more than a slap on the wrist.

I'm curious as to how much longer people are going to watch their "celebrities", "royals" and "politicians" commit heinous crimes without getting jailed. How far gone are people? When will they stand up and demand change? They probably won't, or they would have already. The protests you see on TV aren't organic. If they were, people would be protesting in front of CIA Headquarters or Pfizer, but they aren't. Unless they know the extent of what is happening, few people take initiative and lead the way. I'm not suggesting violence and there are non-violent ways to get it done, which I'll discuss later.

Certain "celebrities" and people close to Hollywood have mentioned human hunting.

Jenna Jameson ✓
@jennajameson

I've heard terrible things about "The Hunt". Children as young as 4. Packs of dobermans. These topics circulate. The first time I heard of these "parties" was when I was in Cannes at the Hotel Du Cap. I wanted not to believe them.

Jenna Jameson, one of the most famous porn-stars of the 90s and 2000s is close friends with certain people that would know about this: Eli Roth, maker of the "Hostel" movies. Marilyn Manson, musician and occultist. Rose McGowan, who has spoken up about elite pedophilia. Asia Argento, Italian actress and daughter of Dario Argento whose movies exposed the Illuminati. Asia Argento has spoken out against Harvey Weinstein. Eli Roth was in a relationship with Peaches Geldof, daughter of Bob Geldof. Peaches was murdered after publicly speaking out about pizzagate and occult child abuse. I'm not going into pizzagate in this book because enough has been written about it elsewhere, except to say that it's all entirely true and the very best example of a hostile, anti-human presence among our most trusted elites.

Macaulay Culkin ✔
@IncredibleCulk

My milkshake brings all the boys to the yard, where I hunt them for sport.

2:16 PM · 6/8/18 · Twitter for Android

858 Retweets and comments **2,725** Likes

Macaulay Culkin is yet another "celeb" who has spoken up against rampant child abuse and child sexual abuse in Hollywood. When he tweets of human hunting, he is probably not joking.

The "mainstream media", ever dishonest, claims human hunting is something the rich will do "in the future". I've read several articles as the one below:

Could Hunger Games become a reality? Hunting HUMANS may be a hobby for the rich in the next 100 years

- By 2200 hunting humans could be televised, and an activity for stag dos
- Changes is natural environment will drive a divide between rich and poor
- Humans in the future will kill others in a 'claimed aim to reduce population size', although there will be a 'perverse thrill and excitement' to it

By SHIVALI BEST FOR MAILONLINE 🐦
UPDATED: 12:54 EDT, 22 June 2016

In reality, it's already been happening. And for how long? I don't wish for a single child or adult to ever be hunted like an animal. Human beings need to stop dividing themselves between race, culture, religion and politics. We need to stick together and not allow our kin to be treated this way.

The "Save the Children" scam

The most anti-human scheme I've ever come across are well-known and generously funded and equipped organizations claiming to help, save and protect children who are actively engaged in the opposite–horrific violence against children. The scam has been run in many variations for a long time and continues, even though it is also regularly exposed.

I could have written an entire chapter on this, exposing at least a dozen famous children's charities, but chose to keep it short to fit this book's scope, using few examples only.

One of the most well-known NGOs is in-fact called "Save the Children". It was founded in 1919 with the supposed goal of "helping improve the lives of children worldwide". The organization is an official consultant to the United Nations and receives Government funding. In 2021, 42 of its top employees were fired after it came to light they had been sexually abusing children for years. I suspect they wouldn't have been fired had the abuse scandal not gone public.

There had been thousands of allegations against the organizations over the years, with very little consequence.

More than 40 Save the Children International staff sacked over abuse, bullying or safeguarding concerns

26 July 2022 by Russell Hargrave

The charity's accounts also show its income rose to nearly £1bn last year

Forty-one members of staff at Save the Children International lost their jobs over abuse, bullying and other safeguarding concerns last year.

Save the Children has a long, long History of very creepy ongoings. No adult should assume they are there to "Save the Children", and yet, despite it all, the organization continues uninterrupted to this day, taking the donations from the naïve populace.

Excerpts from a 2015 BBC article:

The husband of murdered MP Jo Cox, Brendan Cox, has quit two charities he set up in her memory after allegations of sexual assault were made public.

Mr Cox denied assaulting a woman in her 30s at Harvard University in 2015 - but admitted to "inappropriate" behaviour while working for Save the Children.

In 2015 the Mail on Sunday reported that Brendan Cox had stepped down from his position as chief strategist at Save the Children over allegations of "inappropriate behaviour" which he at the time denied.

More details of Mr Cox's alleged behaviour emerged after Oxfam issued its own apology over a sex scandal involving aid workers in Haiti.

Source: https://www.bbc.com/news/uk-43101434

In 2012, the Guardian newspaper, at a time it was still practicing actual journalism, uncovered that the CIA had used "Save the Children" as a front in Afghanistan to stage a fake vaccination drive to infiltrate the inner circle of Osama bin Laden (supposedly).

There is much more on this creepy organization, but let's look at others to establish that "Fake Children's Charity" is an ongoing pattern and a problem that we-the-people need to put an end to.

Once we've established that a Reptilian adversary exists and that it likes children, our first action would have to be to safeguard all places where children are. Daycare centers, schools, playgrounds, swimming facilities, sports centers, scouting organizations, church programs for children, babysitters—all these require closer and more vigilant scrutiny. If you don't believe it, look at the stats, look at the daily "scandals" we hear about in the local news. Look at the police records and court documents. Children are a primary target of the anti-human agenda. Why? Because they are the future of humanity and because their youth is presumably preferred for harvesting.

If you wish to bring awareness to this topic, you don't have to mention Reptilians, of course. I'm sure it would find a wider audience if creepy subterrestrial creatures weren't part of the equation. In fact, you can teach about almost any aspect of this book without Reptilians. Even so, in my mind, the Reptilians are the most likely culprits.

Image: Hindu reptilian-human hybrids.

8

Anti-Reptilian Warfare

So far we have looked at the claims of three authors—Credo Mutwa, Jenny Gosbell and Arizona Wilder. The final author whose claims we'll examine goes by the name of James Bartley. We'll be looking at his book "The Reptilian Mind", which is unique in "reptilian literature", as you'll soon see. The book is open source, available on scribd.com and other websites for free. According to his Bio, Bartley is an "alien abductee" with an interest in intelligence, counterintelligence and special operations who has worked for the Civil Service in an intelligence related capacity.

The words of James Bartley or interviewees in his book are in italic, my commentary in regular font.

Now more than ever we must recognize that there are trigger mechanisms programmed into us which are meant to keep us in perpetual bondage. Whether your particular vulnerability is over-eating, substance abuse (especially crank or crystal meth which is the drug of choice of the dark gods) promiscuity, love obsessions et al., it's all spawned from the same source. This is all predictable. What is also predictable is that there will be "people" in your life who will characterize you as being "fear based" and "spiritually unevolved" merely because you have the self-worth and the self-respect to want to get at the truth of your experiences. Don't listen to these weather-beaten New Age La Dee Dahs. The latter are merely useful idiots. They are members of the "Muppet Show" meant to keep you under the control of the dark side. Now is the time to proclaim our personal sovereignty and throw off the yoke of spiritual enslavement and cosmic vassalage and give our children and our children's children a fighting chance to break out of this mess.

I fully agree that Meth is a portal drug for entities. It degrades a person's character to the point they are ready to become possessed.

Bartley frequently complains about new-agers which he calls "New Age La Dee Dahs". I've made the same observations and have the same complaints, even though mine are less pronounced. For many years, almost every time I've shared something of the bondage and enslavement the ruling elite hold us in, I have some "new ager" commenting that my post, article or book is "fear based". Exposing evil is not fear-based, on the contrary, it's remarkably *courageous*. My conspiracy-minded writings, so far, have garnered me no monetary reward or popularity, on the contrary. Many fans of my books on "the law of attraction" have felt alienated by such writings, have complained about them and even cancelled Business relationships.

At one point in my career I had to choose between pursuing the truth–the nature of reality–or defending my Business interests. If it were my agenda to defend my Business interests, I wouldn't even consider writing this book, nor saying many of the things I've already said. Just the other day I made a post on social media saying that "80% of supplements are a scam". That's the truth as I see it. To the very best of my knowledge and experience. But saying so is very inconvenient for my Business because I have some readers whose livelihood depends on selling supplements. They were not pleased with me posting that. "I've recommended you to hundreds of people and then you trash supplements. They are my only source of income". You see, the problem? Often Business-interest and truth don't agree. But in the grander scheme of things, they do match. To me, running a Business based around timidity and lies is not "success". Success is to speak my truth and still do Business.

Readers who label evil-exposers as "fear based" also have little clue of what these authors go through, in terms of spiritual-warfare.

What we are involved with is Spiritual Warfare and I'll argue that point until someone else is blue in the face. Everything has to first manifest in the unseen realms before they manifest in the visual spectrum, in the spiritual before it manifests in the physical. Look around you: The symbology of the reptilian overlordship is all around. The thought form of reptilians in the mass media is constantly hammering you. Crude and vulgar behaviors are being presented to you in the mass media and the so-called entertainment industry—as if crude and vulgar behavior is The Norm in our society today. The baseness and vulgarity, which is being promoted, is symptomatic of a reptilian influenced society. People are so used to the lies that if they heard the truth, they would probably have an allergic reaction to it!

The reptilians strive to activate that dark serpent seed which is programmed within all of us. The struggle is within. The opposing polarities of Good and Evil are striving to promote certain attributes and behaviors within us. One side wants to corrupt us from within. The other wants us to break out of this spiritual prison. Ultimately it comes down to your own individual choice. I hesitate to use the term "free will" because being an abductee myself I know that I have been manipulated and programmed and it's a constant struggle to overcome all of these hang-ups— but that's what will make the ultimate victory that much greater. I firmly believe in the indomitability of the Human Spirit and I firmly believe that it is in our destiny to achieve Nobility as a race. If we had just been left alone, I am sure we would have reached that level of greatness already but alas, that hasn't been the case.

And if you choose to be a New Age La Dee Dah and your children are having these abductions and you just blow off their concerns as being of no consequence, that makes you in my book a b parent. If people knew what kinds of conditioning and programming are being done to our children by the aliens, people's minds would short circuit instantly to retain their sanity, if nothing else.

These words may seem harsh to some readers, but I fully agree, that's why I reprint them here. We are currently at war. The war is spiritual and physical. It gets tiresome to keep hearing dismissals such as "all is well" and "stop spreading fear-based propaganda". While I believe that all is well in the grand cosmic scheme of things, we still have a responsibility to help eradicate evil from our planet. All is in fact well in my life because I acknowledge and apply the unbending rules of the universe. One of these rules is not to live in denial, to live authentically. Saying that "evil doesn't exist", as I've heard many of my own students tell me, is denialism and will do nothing to increase your awareness. People have told me "Evil is too strong of a word". Knowing what you know from the preceding chapters, is "evil" really too strong of a word? I think not.

Bartley's attitude is a breath of fresh air in an otherwise timid and borderline delusional "Ufology" and "New Age" scene.

...having had a security clearance or prior involvement within the Surface Intelligence/Security and Aerospace communities does not an authority on the UFO subject make.

...Even those who were utilized as operatives within deep black mind control programs involving aliens and have broken free are still trying to piece their fragmented memories together because at that level knowledge is limited by Levels of Awareness and not by clearances. Moreover, the deep black manipulators are loathe to allow these special individuals to slip from their grasp and will strive at all hazards to bring them back under their control. There is a WAR going on.

Again, I fully agree that expertise is determined by level of awareness, not by "clearance" or worldly titles. And consciousness-level is determined by work-on-self, integrity, contemplation, prayer, meditation and study. I am honest for selfish reasons because I know my power to discern true and false depends on it.

The reptilians are paraphysical beings who can alter their vibrational density to operate within the confines of our three dimensional world both in and out of the normal visual spectrum. The reptilians can manipulate the human "dreamscape" and install all manner of conditioning and programming much of which is erotic or perverse in nature. They specialize in manipulating ones dreamscape with erotic imagery specifically designed to promote certain behaviours and alternative lifestyles within a given abductee population. I know of no one else besides our team who is even aware of this very basic and pervasive reptilian programming agenda.

I have also described this in my books. Some beings are paraphysical and can alter their density. This is an important piece of the puzzle and it gets rid of the falsehood that someone is either "physical or spiritual" or "discarnate vs. incarnate".

Bartley's metaphysical comments are spot on. They align with what I have discovered in decades of exploration. Here's somebody that knows what he's talking about from experience, not theory or philosophy. I'm grateful for all I've learned in the decades, it makes discernment of truth vs. falsehood so much easier.

The definition of the word "Lifespan" as we understand the term does not apply to these reptilians who live in their own vibrational density long enough to manipulate countless generations of a given genetic/soul matrix population in our dimension.

The reptilians are master geneticists who have created subservient races of non-human beings to act as Specialists tasked with furthering certain agendas directly impacting the human race including but not limited to genetic and soul matrix manipulation of the abductee population. It is through the latter program that Hosts are created through apparently normal human childbirth. These reptilian hosts are geared to sow confusion, discordance and disinformation amongst the abductee population.

163

Bartley refers to different people being "Hosts" for reptilian entities. Some of these people are human, some are reptilian-human-hybrids. Another word for "hosting" would be possession.

The reptilians do not need spaceships to travel in. They merely create a portal entry in the house of the abductee they need to work with. They literally walk through this space/time opening and appear in your bedroom in full physical density.

It's true that entities can travel without physical spaceships, but this doesn't rule out their use of physical craft.

There is a whole subcategory of abductees, especially female abductees who have been genetically altered to accommodate the needs of their particular reptilian handler. The relationship of the reptilian handler and the female abductee can be likened to that of the Master Adept and the female "Scarlet Woman" within the context of a tantric sexual magickal working.

Women who have been genetically altered by reptilians have certain attributes unique to them. Some of them may develop an acute sense of smell which makes them extremely sensitive to human male pheromones. In some extreme cases they may have been conditioned by their reptilian handlers to lose all sexual interest in human males to the point where they feel nothing but contempt for them. Women having reptilian experiences may go through periods of time when they are craving Vitamin C and will even binge on Tomatoes or Citrus Fruits.

A natural consequence of the sexual encounters between the reptilians and women (some of which have been extremely brutal with the women having their hair pulled and their faces and bodies clawed at and bruised) is that the libido of some women is heightened to an extraordinary degree to the point where their every waking thought is consumed with the notion of sexual intercourse. In some cases this may cause the women to become extremely promiscuous.

In the case of those who do not have partners or are unable to find them they may be compelled to resort to compulsive self-gratification i.e. masturbation. In both instances the aliens "harvest" the sexual energy from these women.

This information was new to me. I hadn't read it anywhere else (and I read a lot!). Bartley's writings are full of unique information. This gives his writings some credibility because dishonest writing is usually nothing more than a watered-down copy of things already written by others. I am familiar with Entities harvesting masturbation-energy from both men and women and have also mentioned this in my writings.

It is not uncommon for light phenomena or even portals to manifest during these women's sexual encounters with men. If the woman is a host for an entity the consciousness of the human female (what's left of it anyway) may depart during sexual intercourse and view the scene from above whilst the reptilian entity takes complete control of the female host. The latter example gives us an example of the androgynous nature of the phenomenon because the reptilian entity or entities within the host are often as not male reptilians and it does not matter in the slightest that the entity is having sex with a human male.

This is not yet widely understood, but it's true that certain sex-rituals are performed by the ruling elite with the goal of manifesting certain entities and the opening of portals. These can sometimes be perceived with the naked eye as orbs and lights.

The reptilians promote the use of certain methamphetamines in particular "Crank" or "Crystal Methedrine" in order to better control and in some cases, to ultimately utilize the abductee as a Host. The latter types of amphetamines have a "sympathetic resonance" to the reptilians and some of their gray workers. Barbara Bartholic has documented dozens of such cases going back to the 1970's whilst most abduction researchers were still learning about "Grays" and "Missing Time" and "Hybrids". In fact most abduction researchers are still stuck in "The Gray Areas." There is a historical basis for the utilization of potions and drugs by countless cultures ancient and modern in order to establish long term contact with non-human intelligences…

Psychedelics also open up these portals but the difference is that the individual can see and perceive the entities. With drugs like speed and meth, the entities remain invisible and can so more easily possess a "host".

Ironically the use (or misuse as it were) of Tantric Sexual Magick is a fundamental part of Black Magick. In other words the Black Magicians know that the feminine generative principle is an immensely powerful force which they exploit for their own evil purposes at the expense of the human race in general and human women in particular. That is what the "V" symbol is all about. A common symbol found on abductees appears to be the Triangle and most so-called abduction researchers regard it as such which again reveals their collective ignorance about these matters. What they are actually looking at is the Trikona. The Trikona (an inverted three sided pyramid or a V) symbolizes the Yoni or the female sexual organ which is the abode of the sleeping fire snake and the source of the kundalini (serpent) energy generated through the Tantric Kaula rites. What salient point do women most often report regarding sexual intercourse with reptilians? They experience the most powerful full body orgasms they have ever had sometimes lasting for hours!

In a Tantric Magickal Working the Adept seeks to activate the kundalini chakra of the female "Scarlet Woman." Once the kundalini is activated and forcefully propels itself through the other chakras finally exiting the crown chakra, the resultant "Ojas" or electromagnetic energy is magickally imbued into metal discs laid atop the middle chakras in order to store the electromagnetic energy.

These metal discs are stored in hermetically sealed containers for later use. These ojas are then imbued into the Adept so at a later time he may impregnate a woman with semen which in turn has been imbued with the power of these ojas in order to procreate a child of special qualities for special purposes.

The latter is just one example of the various usages of the ojas generated by the activation of the kundalini energy by a human Adept. Never mind what the reptilians can do, we're just talking humans here. I should remind the reader that to her dying day Olympia, the mother of Alexander the Great insisted that her son was conceived during sexual intercourse between herself and what she described as a python. Olympia was an initiate of the Dionysian Mystery Schools and had frequently inbibed in hallucinogenics during these rituals many of which involved blood sacrifices, contrary to what some would have you believe. It has also been alleged that Julius Caesar was the product of a union between his mother and an Incubi. I shouldn't have to add anything about the impact these two men had on history in general and western civilization in particular.

I've quoted these sections because they showcase specialized knowledge not found in any other book or movie. I spent some time looking for information on the "ojas metal discs" because I had never heard of them. I found nothing. Not finding any corroboration at all is usually a sign of fabrication. I'd have to assume that the author is lying. It's only through the high-density of other truthful knowledge that I trust the overall message of the author. Had I in fact read his book only ten years ago, I would have surely dismissed it. But the more you know, the more you can categorize.

That is only what is going on in the surface world. Our team is really interested in what is going on in the subterranean world, which has everything to do with abductees. Some of the underground facilities have been described by those who have defected from the Illuminati as "waiting rooms for Hell." I cannot think of a more apt description.

I've gone into some detail of what happens in the subterranean world in my book "Levels of Heaven and Hell". This is where negative entities and Reptilians are stationed both physically and non-physically, as well as in the immediate space around the planet, again both physically and in the astral-realm.

If you call yourself an abduction researcher and you are unaware that:

A) the reptilians and aliens manipulate the dreamscape and condition the physical body to respond to certain stimuli of an erotic or even a perverse nature,

B) that the reptilians promote the use of drugs especially methamphetamine and crank in order to turn an abductee into an energy sucking manipulated puppet and will sometimes host these people to further a particularly violent or sexually perverse agenda or,

C) Can manipulate the health of abductees in myriad ways and have even been responsible for the deaths of abductees or,

D) have actually hosted abductees and researchers alike, then I don't take you seriously. I don't care how popular you are, how many times you've been on the Art Bell show, how pretty your website is, how many books you've sold, how massive your ego is or how long you've been playing Big Shot Researcher.

I fully agree. As a teenager I read at least thirty books on UFOs or UFO-Abductions. I finally gave up on the subject because none of the well-known researchers were going into aspects that were known to me. They weren't talking about subterranean realms, about MILABs, reptilians, astral and dream-scape manipulation, flying saucers manufactured by the Government and many other very important aspects. They talked about "space brothers" who were there to warn us about environmental hazards (as if we needed aliens for that) or about the "journey of enlightenment" the abductee is on, as if being taken against your will has anything to do with enlightenment.

Likewise, all of this metaphysical new age UFO related information serves as the literary version of what I call "MTV Programming." MTV programming is that type of television eye sore which consist of having countless unrelated images randomly juxtaposed and flashed in lightning sequence across the television screen which ultimately serves to fragment the conscious awareness of the viewer if they subject themselves to this type of entertainment (or entrainment) for too long.

The long term effect of New Age Metaphysical thought upon the conscious and subconscious mind of those within the muppet show is exactly the same, because they spend all there waking hours dwelling on metaphysical abstractions and philosophies instead of what's going on in the real physical world,- thus losing what the military fighter pilots refer to as "situational awareness." They become lost in a spiritual haze of their own making.

Having coached people since the early 1990s, I've probably met tens of thousands of people. My primary observation is that humans weaken themselves the most by being lost in thought rather than action, concept rather than experience, opinions rather than skills.

It must be understood by the reader that there is PHYSICALITY in the astral dreamscape. Notice how a reptilian can seduce a woman or sodomize a man through layers of bedsheets, comforters and night clothes. They densify only those parts of their anatomy where and when they need to. They can be invisible in the visible spectrum and yet conduct forcible rape or sodomy that is a very real physical traumatic event to the human. The woman may see only an illusion of a famous entertainer or musical artist...

Astral Sex is physical sex. Although it may sound like a paradox, it isn't if you understand how frequency and resonance works. Many women wake up in the morning after being raped by a reptilian feeling soreness in their vaginas and sometimes in their rectums as well.

As unfamiliar this may sound, I've heard "this kind of thing" from people. The sense that they had been sexually attacked at night by an unknown entity. Such people ask me questions like "Is it possible that there are astral beings trying to have sex with me?" and "Why do I wake up with the feeling I have been sexually molested? There is nobody else in my house". The ancients spoke of "incubus" and "succubus" entities that sexually abuse humans. Unlike James Bartley I don't believe we fall victim to "this kind of thing" randomly, it requires a weakened energy-field.

Pedophilism is promoted much the same way as mentioned above. A man may find himself in an erotic dreamscape scenario with a woman. He begins to caress and fondle the woman. He is in a highly aroused state of being. The woman he is with contrives to make the man lie on his back and she mounts him while he is in a fully aroused state. However, the moment the woman mounts him and he penetrates her vagina, the woman shapeshifts into a young child. Sometimes the woman will shapeshift into the man's own daughter. Other times the man may be kissing and caressing a woman and then the woman will shapeshift into a young teenage boy. The man will be taken aback by this sudden change of events and pull back. Meanwhile a voice in his mind will be encouraging him to continue caressing this young boy. The voice will tell him things like "Go ahead. Its just a dream. Go ahead, no one will know." The male's erogenous zone is being manipulated by the reptilians all the while in order to keep him in this highly aroused state. In the case of a female abductee, she may be having an erotic dream with her "ideal man" or someone she has a crush on in real life. One thing leads to another and right before she begins performing fellatio on the dream guy, he shapeshifts into a young boy or in some cases, into her own son. There are numerous variations of this form of astral dreamscape manipulation. Suffice it to say that it is all meant to encourage that individual to begin indulging himself or herself in pedophilism.

Again, as far-fetched as this might sound to most readers, dreamscape manipulation by lower astral entities is "a thing" and this sounds precisely like the kind of agenda lower astrals would have. Even so, it's not that easy to manipulate a person who is on a medium to high consciousness level. On dreamscape, I detect attempted manipulation fairly quickly and end it. Sexual harassment of men, women and children however, is widely reported as one of the common traits of Reptilians.

If you look back in America's history, you will find that the further you go back into time, the more likely you will find that Americans owned and operated their own businesses. Whether these businesses were Farms, Mills, Tanneries or Shops, often as not the businesses were family owned and passed down from generation to generation. For those who didn't inherit a family run business, an entrepreneur would often set up his own business in whatever trade that best suited his skills and temperament. Again, the readers can test this for themselves. Find out what your grandfathers and great-grandfathers did for a living and you will find that most of them were SELF EMPLOYED.

A very valid point. What happened to us? Not only were most of us self-employed, we also self-sufficiently grew food rather than taking it from strangers. There has been an influence in society that has worked toward making us increasingly more dependent on external factors. The dependence-agenda continues. At the time of this writing, there are plans to make currency completely digital and making our money subject to "social credit scores".

The slowness with which these things are happening, reminds me of the frog in the boiling water. If you heat up the pot too quickly, the frog gets scared and jumps out. But if you heat it up very slowly it's not noticed, and the frog gets used to the heat.

First he began to have thoughts about harming his own beloved cat. Different methods of killing and maiming the cat went through his mind including flushing it down the toilet and breaking its legs and mutilating it. He was shocked by these feelings because he loved the cat. The reader must understand that reptilians detest CATS. CATS are the best reptilian detectors and reptilian busters known to mankind. They have been known to wake up female abductees moments before the onset of a reptilian abduction or rape.

Having two cats of my own, I am certain that they sense or even see the presence of entities. Oftentimes they stare or meow at things we don't see.

I mentioned that I'd like to meet some of the women in her group and discuss the reptilian and military aspect of their experiences. She peppered her conversation with constant references to her "Guides" as in "My Guides told me this" and "My guides told me that...." She must have said that about six or seven times. Soon the long holiday weekend was over and we went our separate ways. A couple of days later I received a telephone call from

Effluvia. Here is where all the problems started since I didn't realize at the time that Effluvia was hosted by a number of entities including a dominant male reptilian.

The continuous reference to "my guides" and "angel guides" and "soul guides" in the new-age scene is questionable to me. Who is to say whether these are lower-astral spirits or not? The fact is that you are a powerful being and don't require the assistance of lesser entities.

In a future work I will elaborate on this concept but suffice it to say for now, MILABS used as "Astral Operators" can be made to perform as a "multi-task platform." They can not only remotely view a distant location, they can act as a psychic "comm-link" to numerous other astral operators on the same "op." MILABS in the Astral Operator Mode have been used to identify targets on the ground that are subsequently taken out with smart munitions like JDAMS. MILABS used as Astral Operators have identified the locations of groups of Taliban and Al-Qaeda members living in underground tunnel complexes in Afghanistan such as those built by former CIA asset Osama Bin Laden's family construction firm. Once these underground hide-outs had been conclusively identified by MILABS, the precise location of the tunnel complexes are attacked with "Bunker Busters" delivered by strike aircraft. Likewise, special operations forces are sometimes sent to reconnoitre tunnel systems previously identified as Taliban and Al-Qaeda hiding places by MILABS. Of course the pilots delivering the smart munitions and the bunker busters, as well as the spec ops troops entering the cave and tunnel systems would never dream that some of the intel obtained for their missions came from MILABS.

More than a decade after Bartley published his book it became publicly known that the Taliban entertained a vast network of Tunnel systems.

U.S. military drops "Mother of All Bombs" on ISIS tunnel complex

On April 13, 2017, American forces in Afghanistan drop one of the largest non-nuclear weapons ever used by the U.S. military. The "Mother of All

Bombs" hits an Islamic State tunnel complex with power equal to 11 tons of explosives. More than 90 Islamic State militants died in the bombing.

Source: https://www.history.com/this-day-in-history/mother-of-all-bombs-afghanistan

Throughout his book, Bartley displays an offensive and optimistic attitude toward combating reptilians. As far back as the 1990s, he spoke without shame or equivocation on the subject. My verdict is: More people like him are needed.

9

The Owl Cult That Runs The World

This article originally appeared on my website www.falsehistory.net. I include it here so that you learn more about the ruling elite and their symbols, their History and what it's all got to do with those "fallen angels".

In my books I documented a world-empire of ancient-German-speaking people. Did these people build the Pyramids, Cathedrals and other grandness? Possibly. Their kingdom was destroyed, their buildings blasted to pieces or buried under water, sand and mud. Only a few remain. Here's a 1572 map showing Cairo (here called Cairo Babylon) with 12 Pyramids atop hills. Only three remain, the rest are destroyed and/or buried.

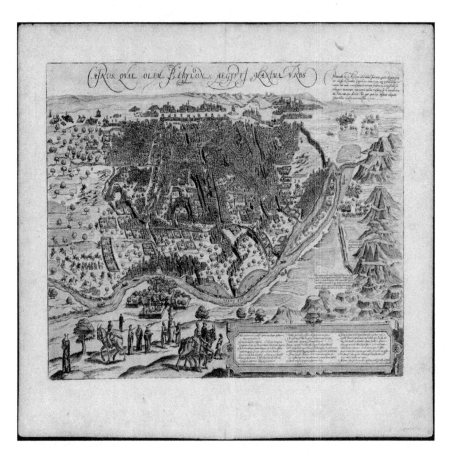

From the fertile lands turned into barren desert, we get legends about Atlantis, Lemuria and in more recent years, Tartaria. The defeated people became known as "indigenous tribes" while the French, British, German, Dutch and other armies travelled the world to occupy their territories and erase any remains of their former identity. The native Americans, the Aborigines of Australia, the Maori of New Zealand, the indigenous of Siberia—no matter where I looked, I found traces of the same ancient German language. I learned as much about these forgotten people as I could. Their main theme was that they revered a "Holy Owl". This *Wai Ulu* and *Wai Uhu* kept coming up in place names, legends, stories and religious texts of the ancients. You can read about it in my books *Extraterrestrial Linguistics* and *The Secret History of Ancient Polynesia*. Or you can find traces of this forgotten truth in very old newspaper articles:

The Owl in History.

The owl was in former times generally regarded as an omen of misfortune or death; but as the Egyptians represented Minerva under the form of an owl, the Athenians, who were under the care of this goddess, looked upon the appearance of the owl as a favorable omen. It therefore formed upon the ancient coins referred to the symbol of Athens and her foreign possessions. The Chinese and the Tartars have also held the owl in high esteem. The first named used to wear owl's feathers in their caps, and some Tartar tribes still worship idols made like owls.—New York Weekly.

If the resolution does not allow you to read this, the relevant sentence says "The Chinese and the Tartars have also held the owl in high esteem. The first named used to wear owl's feathers in their caps and some Tartar tribes still worship idols make like owls."

The fascinating thing is that the owl-worshippers are still around! Instead of having been defeated, they seem to have retaken control of the world. In the old days, they ruled the world openly, today they rule it secretly.

The image below is the Owl statue at *Bohemian Grove* in California. For a long time, the world's elite from politics, industry, banking and entertainment met here once a year for strange performances and rituals, as if trying to revive the "old religion".

The image below is the area of the Capitol in Washington D.C. shaped as an Owl, built in 1793.

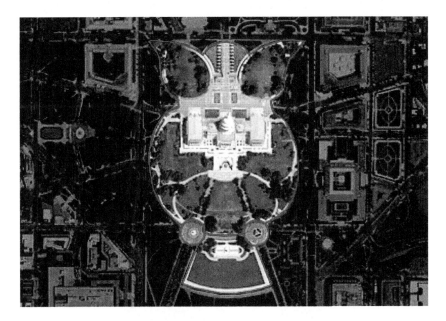

How many people knew that our elites are into this Owl thing? Yes, the Owl is also perched on every 1-Dollar Bill:

On May 1st of 1776, a secret society called "The Illuminati" was founded in Ingolstadt, Germany by Adam Weishaupt. Their declared goal was the infiltration of all sectors private and public to final world domination within only a few centuries. This was their Owl-themed Logo:

The Owl Logo can be found across many corporate buildings, Government offices and Universities, so apparently the Illuminati accomplished their mission.

My research in *Extraterrestrial Linguistics* revealed that the ancients believed Owls can communicate with beings in other realms. This has always been the primary goal of various occultic rituals–the summoning of entities outside of our Dimension.

I first learned about "the Owl thing" in 1992, while watching the TV-Series "Twin Peaks". There, a Giant appears to FBI Agent Dale Cooper and tells him that "the Owls are not what they seem".

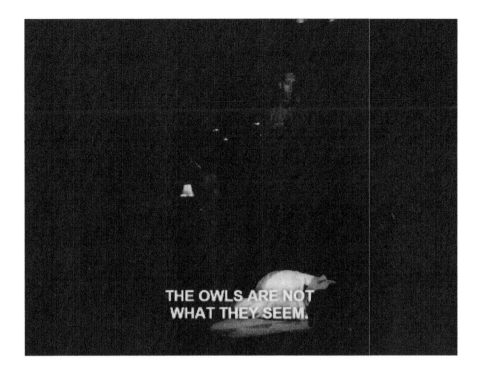

Later in the show, we see the Owl is a shapeshifting Demon, turning from a possessing entity named Bob into an Owl. In another scene, Owls are associated with extraterrestrials. Finally, a native American Elder sees the Owl symbol and says that it represents a great evil.

The famous TV-Series, poorly understood by mainstream audiences, is really about demonic possession that leads to sadistic murder, human trafficking and other anti-human behavior. We're shown an invisible world behind ours from which great evil and great good arise. The Owl rules the underworld (which is a figurative underworld, as in world of crime, and a literal underworld as in below Earth).

The subsequent series, the 2018 "Twin Peaks–The Return", confirms that the TV-show is really about these nature-of-reality issues and not a mere "crime show".

Nuclear explosions create a crystal called icosahedrite which are shaped like pentagrams. Both pentagrams and nuclear explosions are used to "open portals" to summon "entities" from other realms (as also shown in the TV Series "Twin Peaks - The Return").

www.falsehistory.net

Source/Reference: https://www.syfy.com/syfy-wire/a-nuclear-test-creates-a-forbidden-crystal-this-is-the-fivefold-wayhj

There is a scene in Twin Peaks, where the first atomic explosion, causes legions of entities to crawl onto Earth. The explosion took place at the 33rd Latitude at a place now called the Trinity site. Is there any significance to this number? Yes, a very ancient significance.

It goes back to the Bible where it says that when Lucifer fell to Earth, he took 1/3 of the angels with him. Another way of saying 1/3 is 33% or more specifically 33.33 %. Ever since that event, the fallen ones identify themselves with the number 33.

The Bible says that Lucifer landed on Mount Hermon, which is, of course, also exactly on Latitude 33.33. What a "coincidence". Where is Mount Hermon? It's a "U.N. Buffer Zone" between Israel, Syria and Lebanon. It's one of the many places on Earth not run by a single nation.

In a move that surprised the world, information about the Owl-Cult was broadcast to hundreds of Millions in 2017. Military people around Donald Trump, calling themselves "Q, started posting about the Owl-folks on a message board called 8Chan. The Q-movement spread like fire and for the first time in hundreds of years, millions of normies got clued in on the ancient ways of the fallen ones. Then, it became the most censored topic of all time. The Government tried to take down the 8chan Internet-Domain. The owner, Jim Watkins, had to go testify before Congress. Ultimately, they could not take down the site because, as researchers discovered, the Domain was run by the Department of Defense. It's a case of one branch of Government not knowing what the other is doing. Trump and his army of Q-researchers were ultimately removed from Facebook, Twitter, YouTube, Google Search and many other platforms. The topic was made not to exist, so that the normies could continue living their pampered worldview. It was the first time a sitting President had been aggressively prevented from speaking to the public. The Owl-Cultists awoke to what was going on a little late, but when they did, the backlash was ferocious. Trump's presidential win in 2020 was taken away and the Covid-plandemic created.

When I read the Q posts back in 2017, I recognized the topic, because I had been studying the Owl-Worship Mythology for years. What struck me the most is that "Q" kept referring to them as Owl / Y.

Q !ITPb.qbhqo ID: pOV0fY+r No.150412315 🖻 ▉   **184**
Nov 21 2017 22:07:58 (EST)

Their need for symbolism will be their downfall.
Follow the Owl & Y head around the world.
Identify and list.
They don't hide it.
They don't fear you.
You are sheep to them.
You are feeders.
Godfather III.
Q

> **Q** !ITPb.qbhqo ID: CJqu8olu No.150424047 ☑ 🏴   **189**
> Nov 21 2017 23:52:02 (EST)
>
> Identify symbolism (Owl / Y).
> Which performers/celebs supported HRC during the election?
> Who performed during her rallies?
> What jewelry and/or tattoos present?
> What other events do they attend together?
> What does HRC represent to them?
> What celebrities have owl / Y head symbols?
> What politicians have owl / Y head symbols?
> What powerful people have owl / Y head symbols?
> What powerful groups have owl / Y head symbols?
> Why are they worn/shown openly?
> Their need for symbolism will be their downfall.

Source: qanon.pub

This is *exactly* how the ancient German-speaking people referred to their Owl. The word "Wai" pronounced "Y" means "sacred" or "holy" to them. The Y-Owl is the "Holy Owl". I'm the first and so far only author to discover and share the real and ancient meaning of Y/Owl symbolism. I'm not saying that to brag, I'm saying it to complain: So *few people* know or care about this stuff. How do people ever expect to take back their planet if 99% of the people don't know the first thing about the ones running the show?

The Owl "is a thing" among elites. So is the letter Y. And the number 33. I've had several encounters in my life with these people, which I'll share some time in the distant future. Here's one of Hillary Clinton's many very revealing emails that were leaked by Julian Assange, who got a lifelong prison sentence for leaking these matters.

 WikiLeaks   Leaks   News   About   Partners

UNCLASSIFIED U.S. Department of State Case No. F-2014-20439 Doc No. C05791990 Date: 12/31/2015

RELEASE IN
PART B5

From: H <hrod17@clintonemail.co>
Sent: Saturday, February 26, 2011 3:04 PM
To: 'sullivanjj@state.gov'

Subject: Re: Latest

Ok--and Minerva agrees.

From: Sullivan, Jacob J [mailto:SullivanJJ@state.gov]
Sent: Saturday, February 26, 2011 02:44 PM

To: H
Subject: Latest

Do you think the last paragraph violates the owl/minerva rule?

They are fine with the last paragraph.

STATEMENT BY SECRETARY CLINTON

Readers of *Extraterrestrial Linguistics* will recall my mention of Min-erva, a reference to an extraterrestrial place called Min.

This is Minerva, according to Wikipedia:

"*Owl of Minerva*" redirects here. For the scientific journal, see *The Owl of Minerva (journal)*.

In Greek mythology, a little owl (*Athene noctua*) traditionally represents or accompanies Athena, the virgin goddess of wisdom, or Minerva, her syncretic incarnation in Roman mythology.[2] Because of such association, the bird—often referred to as the "**owl of Athena**" or the "**owl of Minerva**"—has been used as a symbol of knowledge, wisdom, perspicacity and erudition throughout the Western world.[3][4]

Classical World [edit]

Ancient Greece [edit]

Further information: Athena

The reasons for the association of Athena and the owl are uncertain. Some mythographers, such as David

And does that image of an owl or an AOL remind you of something? Why yes, the very first big internet company:

The most popular "Illuminati" (Illu-Min-ati) symbol is the eye in the triangle, the second most popular is now the Owl. The first big Internet company somehow managed to get both into the same Logo just to make sure there is absolutely no doubt which team they are on. Every large international company in existence is eager and excited to advertise their allegiance. I could write a book with thousands of examples of this, but I'll provide just one more in Paramount, one of the biggest film companies in the world:

Anyone get the reference? Maybe if you count the number of stars.

It's 22 stars. Get it now? No?

Think Mount Hermon.

Lucifer took 33.33 % of the Angels, which were 22 angels. The Book of Enoch names each of these 22 "superstars" by name. When you're in a movie theater and watch the Paramount Logo take shape, notice how the stars are falling from the sky and then landing atop the mountain.

Around the time of the Q-postings, the Internet was also flooded with memes, videos and posts about "Tartary" or "Tartaria". Every time I posted something online about fake History, someone would comment "Tartaria!" or something of that nature. It usually went along with "mud flood" and "flat earth" type information. Just like the Q-stuff, the Tartaria stuff wasn't organic. I could tell because it was pushed so strongly. All these social media accounts with hundreds of thousands of followers sprang up. Even if I opened YouTube on a neutral browser (one I wasn't using), Videos on that topic were being suggested to me. Why is this shown to normies? And why did that same YouTube not allow Videos on the Trump election fraud for years? By seeing *what is pushed vs. what is censored* by global-power-players you learn the most.

People thought these revelations on Fake History were part of "the Great Awakening" to take down the dark side. But what if it was that very dark-side that was destroyed? If the dark-side were more candid, they might come out and say this:

"Yeah, look, we were imprisoned here against our will, by the Creator of this realm. So, we said, ok, whatever. Let's make the best of it and build a really nice world. Utopia. Heaven on Earth. And then he comes down and destroys everything we built, because he can't tolerate any greatness besides his own. So, we're really pissed off and we'll now do everything in our power to destroy his people and his creation."

If the light-side were more candid and quit beating around the bush, they might say:

"Here's the thing. They hate humans. The Creator imbued them with special powers while at the same time demoting these lizard folk. Ever since then, in their envy, they are trying to debase humanity with different schemes, while imprisoned down here. But the Creator allows that, because it puts humans to the test and helps them exercise their free choice. The Creator wants to see who will choose to side with them vs. him. This realm isn't even meant to be Paradise anymore, more like a Training camp. So, toughen up."

With that clarified, everyone would understand what's going on and we could all move on to something better.

But with no clarification from "higher ups" our only option left is that we ourselves BECOME the higher ups and bring a more candid and transparent culture into this world.

10

Things They'll Never Tell You About Jeffrey Epstein

*This chapter originally appeared as an article on my website falsehistory. net.
I include it here to shed further light on the occultic nature of the ruling elite.*

Mainstream News vs. Reality

In the mainstream, the Jeffrey Epstein case was about a rare child-sex-trafficking and blackmail operation on rich people, somehow involving Bill Clinton, Bill Gates, Prince Andrew, Les Wexner and other Epstein buddies. I chose not to write on it, assuming the *occult-spiritual aspects* would come to light because so many researchers were combing through the case. Now, 5 years later, I realize the deeper layers never surfaced. The case is forgotten to the mainstream mind, filed away as "some sex-blackmail operation". But that's only 10% of the story and as such, *False History* by omission.

The real story is this: There is a *secret religion* around energy-harvesting that Epstein and friends follow. Epstein is only one of many. One scapegoat was jailed but what about hundreds of others?

And why does their entire belief-system remain unmentioned? It's called *the old religion, the cabal, the illuminati, the left-hand path, luciferians* and many other names. In this article I simply refer to them as *the cult*. The cult is not limited to one country or ethnicity, they operate everywhere.

The real story is these politicians and celebrities are not victims of Epstein's charm and persuasion, they are themselves *cult members* who *knowingly and willingly* participated in "certain activities" knowing they are being filmed. It's known and accepted that the films are used as "insurance" by the cult.

The real story is that they are obsessed with symbols, numbers, planetary alignments, sun, moon, stars, times, dates, names, spells, sigils, colors, invocations, compass orientation, longitude and latitude. They are desperate to keep their "religion" secret because it would shed light on *who* we are, *where* humanity really is, how History is a fabrication and how we can exit the matrix. It would reveal that our "leaders" answer to non-human Beings. Mainstream reports are just narrative-control.

Spirits of the North and South

After Epstein was arrested, there were Videos by random people illegally entering the Island. For a short period, the Island was almost unattended. One of the more famous ones can be found here:

https://www.youtube.com/watch?v=VmgSM7lWRts

In this video, the two brave boatsmen wonder why a Billionaire couldn't afford to have a real door on his Temple, why it's painted on:

They conclude that it's "like a movie set". But that's the wrong conclusion. There is a real, glass door on the other side of the building and there are also submarine and subterranean entrances. Epstein lived a life of extreme luxury, he wasn't trying to save money by painting a door.

The door is *not for physical beings, it's for spirits*. Painting an open or a closed door on a temple to either invite or ward off spirits is ancient practice that is not well known today, but I know about it because I spent years studying mythology.

For members of "the old religion", everything has meaning, and every detail is accounted for. The design is not just random:

People have speculated that it's modeled after the Greek Flag because pedophilia is more permissible in ancient Greece, but that's not it.

You have seven levels of water and air, representing seven levels of Heaven, each separated by a cosmic ocean. It's also the polarity of *electric air* and *magnetic water* (spiritually speaking) and the unity of the two in the keystone topping the arch. The eighth blue stripe is the *keystone*. That's the arch-on or god-like status these people are trying to achieve with their misguided rituals and which they display through their arch-itecture.

The door is painted on and it's shut. The building is aligned on the North-South axis. If you visit Google Maps and input "Little St. James Island" (even that name has meaning to them) you'll find it's aligned not with the geographic north pole but with the *geomagnetic north pole.*

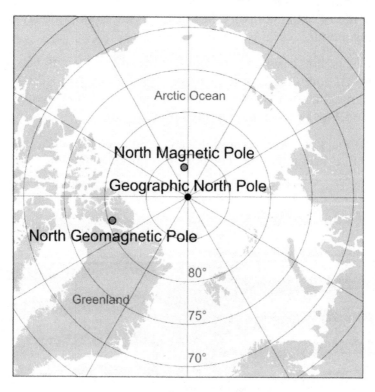

Is it possible that, before the land was purchased, someone drew a line to check whether it aligns?

Here it is on Google Earth:

So the shut door is pointing north. What does it mean? I'm familiar with this from ancient celtic (atlantean) practice. There are tens of thousands of ruins of celtic enclosures strewn across Europe. Archaeologists have found that *not a single one of them ever had doors to the north*. The entrances face to the south. From their mythology we learn that, to them, north represents darkness and evil. Symbolically shutting the door to the North is supposed to keep "the northern spirits" out. The glass door on the other side of Epstein's Temple does open to the South. Other traditions claim that the North represents the angelic realm and any manifestation travels from the north and crystallizes or manifests in the South. In a reversal of the doctrine just described, they believe that the "Northern Star" is reached via north pole and that this is a bridge to higher realms.

On each side of the north of the temple, stood golden statues of Poseidon and Hades as well as two tall birds on the roof, one looking east, the other west. These guards are not present on the south side. The south side is unguarded.

Care to guess what the red lines around the temple mean? Maybe this helps:

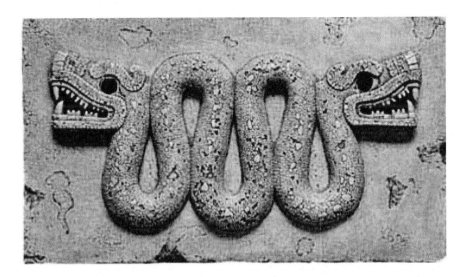

The purpose is to let certain entities pass and keep others out. The lines are *orientation* for spirits. In the astral-realm it's difficult to read words in this realm, so they display large symbols that can easily be seen from the air.

Here, the serpent energy is allowed to pass (or energy in general - any sort of electricity comes in a serpentine wave-form). As I've explained elsewhere, the whole purpose of their ritualistic abuse is to harvest energy or summon entities that assist them in gaining worldly power or travel to other realms. The "workings" done in this temple attract a variety of entities, but not all are welcome. Certain entities are captured inside the boxes, but the serpent is led first to the shut door and then to the side of the house. At the end of its trail it finds a burnt offering:

Epstein of Atlantis

The image below is Epstein's Zorro Ranch in New Mexico. Notice the concentric circle symbol:

From above:

Mainstream journalists claim it's a landing platform for helicopters. That may be one purpose. But it reminds me of something else.

I used WayBackMachine to find a copy of my old, since deleted website "Ancient Atlantis". I got this screenshot from it:

Remember when I *abruptly* deleted the website (I think it was in 2017) saying "it attracts creepy people"? Well, now you know what kind of people it attracted and why.

I chose the symbol because I read somewhere that it's an ancient logo of Platos' Atlantis. I didn't know it also has a special meaning to *the cult*. I'm still not entirely sure what it means to them.

Considering they align their temples just like the Atlantean celts, are they trying to revive Atlantis and it's "old religion"?

Another guess is that the circles center is a vortex or crossing of ley lines or longitude/latitude lines. The cult are *very particular* about this kind of stuff.

I drew a straight line from the circle to the Trinity Site in New Mexico (the site of the explosion of the first atomic bomb) and got 111 miles distance. 1+1+1 = Trinity.

Sure, that may be a coincidence, but the idea of "Trinity" and "merging of polarity" is important to these people, as you will see in a later part of this article. You'll find polarity and trinity in much of Epstein's personal symbolism. Atop his roof there is one bird looking east and the other looking west and at the center a golden dome. That's one example.

The detonation of the nuclear bomb was also important to them, they understood it as an opening of portals to other Dimensions.

There are many others like Epstein

The image below was found hanging in Epstein's NYC mansion. In front of George Bush we see two broken towers while he is holding a paper plane. The symbolism is that the paper couldn't have the power to bring down the two towers. Or, as many engineers say: The buildings must have been rigged with explosives.

"But George Bush was never affiliated with Epstein!" some say. Well, not publicly. But Bush was close friends with Peter Nygard, another child abusing and trafficking "business magnate" (ever notice how the word magnate and magnet sound the same? Not a coincidence). The finnish-canadian Peter Nygard didn't make as much news as Epstein, the story was successfully suppressed. Here's Nygard with the senior Bushes:

Bill Gates insists he had "no idea" what Epstein does, despite his dozens of publicly known visits. I guess he also had "no idea" what his pal Peter Nygard does:

Convicted adult and child trafficker Peter Nygard with Globalist Elite member Bill Gates. Nygard is called "The Canadian Jeffrey Epstein."

This is Bill Clinton in a blue lady's dress and red shoes, another picture hanging in Epstein's NYC mansion. Epstein is showcasing some kind of leverage, perhaps blackmail, over these people.

The Subterranean and Submarine Cult

The statue of Poseidon, in front of the Temple, represents the submarine. The statue of Hades represents the subterranean.

The temple was only the cap of the Pyramid. There is always an underground aspect when it comes to the cult.

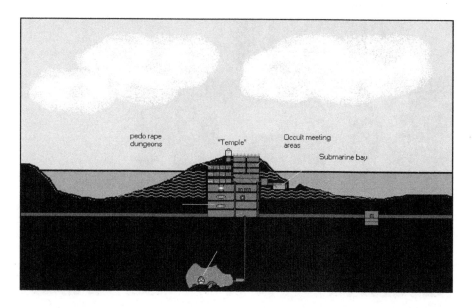

This picture, picked off the Internet, is probably not accurate. But the idea of underground layers is correct. Some believe there was a subway leading from the Island to continental U.S. It's also rumored that all the intercontinental phone and internet cables pass right below the Island.

According to eyewitnesses, Zorro Ranch also had several underground layers, the first layer being a strip club. That's why the property is built atop a hill. Good luck trying to find any of this in the "meticulously researched" Netflix documentary.

It's known that Little St. James had a submarine docking station because celebrities in submarines were pictured on their way to the Island, before it fell into disrepute. After its purpose became known, to the great surprise of all, celebrities quickly went silent about their visits to it. Here's the worlds most famous physicist, Stephen Hawking on his way to the island:

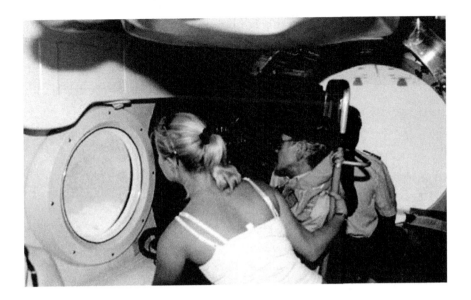

Source: https://www.telegraph.co.uk/news/science/stephen-hawking/11340494/Stephen-Hawking-pictured-on-Jeffrey-Epsteins-Island-of-Sin.html

It's probably the reason that Ghislaine Maxwell got her submarine license.

Her "Terramar" project (see logo below) was claimed to be about "saving the oceans" and counteracting climate change. In reality, it was about trafficking children for abuse.

The logo reminded me of the symbol created by "an apparition of the Virgin Mary" from more than a hundred years ago. Mary appeared to a girl and told her to create a medal of this design and that it would bring miracles and healing to anyone who wore it. It's called "the miraculous medal":

The Terramar logo is exactly the same, except that the top of the cross, symbolizing God or Heaven, is cut off. Another uncanny coincidence?

Epstein's Names, Numbers and Colors

Many of the pictures in Epstein's mansions were blurred or blacked out due to pornographic material, but the images that weren't censored are strange enough. Can you see the Polarity-Trinity concept? A mirror on the left and on the right and the entity in the center. The chimney shows a spiral to the left and a spiral to the right and a chalice at the center. Nothing is random.

The image below is from Epstein's NYC mansion. The framed eyes in the upper corner of the room are reportedly real human eyeballs. This is common practice among practitioners of "the old religion". It's supposed to give you psychic surveillance of your property. Notice also that there's not just one statue below the painting, but two, again for polarity, just like each lamp comes in pairs.

They communicate through codes, colors and symbols. They like chequered floors, red-white stripes and blue-white stripes all of which have meaning in their cosmology.

Blood-vein aesthetic is common and used in their fashion, art and furniture:

Of course there is not just one lamp, there are two lamps flanking the center sofa. The lamps themselves show an upward and downward spiral. Just like there are two star-pillows there and four blood-vessel pillows on the outside. The exact symmetry of everything points toward control-freak mentality.

Notice the medicine cabinet here. One vortex to the right, one to the left. A shiny object at the top, flanked by two lights. Three beings on each side. These are *choices* that Epstein made for *purposes* to do with their religious beliefs.

Notice anything out of the ordinary in Epsteins office room below?

No? Then I guess anyone has two equidistant crystal scrying balls flanking animal horns on their desk. And why am I not surprised that the pillars in the walls come in pairs?

The island is full of small demon statues, placed at specific places for entities to occupy:

Both Epsteins Palm Beach mansion (photo below) and his Virgin Islands Temple had a dentist's chair.

I used to see images of the dentist's chair in the Temple, but they've been scraped from the Internet. Why would Epstein have dentist chairs as a centerpiece of his temple? Is dentistry a hobby of his? I don't know. But I'm familiar with 18th and 19th Century accounts of "hypnotists" and "occultists" using them for mkultra-style drugging and torture.

In the background of the image we see a statue with an erect penis. In the foreground we see an airplane with the sigil JE on it, for Jeffrey Epstein.

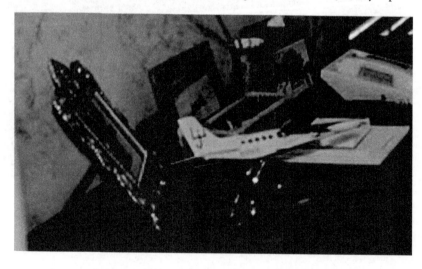

There is also a large version of this plane:

What is a Sigil? It's letters or words strung together so that the conscious mind can no longer discern the word or letters. The purpose of this is to imprint the message into the subconscious whilst "bypassing the censor" (the conscious mind). It's somewhat common among occultists.

Wikipedia:

It's also common for them to have *miniature versions or "graven images" of objects and people* in their possession. It enables them to practice sympathetic magic (quantum entanglement, voodoo). They believe that what they do with the mock-up version also happens to the real version. This is why Epstein reportedly had chess pieces of each of his staffers (see image below, from Epsteins NYC mansion).

A chessboard with each piece modeled after one of his staffers

One visitor told <u>The New York Times</u> that inside the mansion, at the end of the stairwell, there was a chessboard with custom figures. Each piece was reportedly modeled after one of his staffers.

Also, again, do you see the Trinity concept on the table in the image above? I have yet to read *any* article mainstream or alternative or any "conspiracy" article that points out this blatant fact. There's also a bull, but talking about that would overstretch this article.

I checked the Sotheby's sales price of the Zorro ranch (which still isn't sold) and noticed that whoever is selling the house wants people to know that it's 33,339 square feet.

49 Zorro Ranch Road
Stanley, New Mexico, 87056 United States

PRICE

$18,000,000

INTERIOR

33,339 Sq Ft.

I doubt that it's actually 33,339 sq ft. I think this is just more symbolic communication between numbers-crazed cultists.

Want to take any guesses what the solar dome atop the temple means and what its function is? I know it, but I don't want to say everything because it deprives you of the opportunity to think for yourself.

And why would you need a large "solar clock" on your property? Is it just "eccentric art" as mainstream journalists say?

Or maybe it's because they believe that certain dimensional doorways are the most easily accessible at specific times?

A closer look reveals benches for sitting and rocks at specific places. What compass direction is this pointing toward? Which planets are symbolized? What do the people who participate there, do with this? It's not just art. I'll leave it up to you to figure out.

We even find the pyramidal "trinity" line on Epsteins New Mexico property:

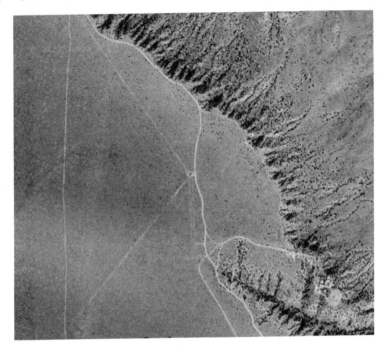

I'll also leave this one, from Epstein Island, for decoding to you:

Mainstream Misdirection

It's Ghislaine Maxwell on the left. But who is that beside her?

Any guesses? Take a close look before you read on. A very close look.

If I don't tell you what mainstream news claims, you probably guessed that this is Maxwell's daughter. They have the exactly same teeth, the same lips, nearly the same eyes and the same nose.

Mainstream media called her Sarah Kellen and turned her into another one of many Maxwell victims. Does she look like a victim to you?

The purpose of this subterfuge is obvious: Since mommy is in jail, someone is needed to continue the family Business.

Many genuine victims have come forward, but I don't believe Kellen is one of them. I also have my doubts about Sarah Ransome.

You can find a video of Mrs. Ransome online. I believe there is only one video of her, in which she calls out Jeffrey Epstein. After that, she was never heard of again.

What she's saying in the video is true, many were used and abused. But honestly: Have you ever heard of someone named Ransome?

Dictionary

Definitions from <u>Oxford Languages</u> · <u>Learn more</u>

 ran·som

noun

a sum of money or other payment <u>demanded</u> or paid for the release of a <u>prisoner</u>.
"the kidnappers demanded a ransom"

Similar: payoff payment price

verb

obtain the release of (a <u>prisoner</u>) by making a payment <u>demanded</u>.
"the lord was captured in war and had to be ransomed"

That's almost like coded language to someone, saying they want money in exchange for the release of Ghislaine or Jeffrey. Or maybe it's about the daughter "Sarah Kellen". Sarah means princess and Kellen is ancient German for slender. "Slender Princess". Maybe it's indicating that a ransom needs to be paid for Sarah to be free. It appears that the ransom wasn't paid because mainstream media later changed their story from "Sarah Kellen was a victim" to "Sarah Kellen was a co-conspirator".

It's almost like one faction of the cult is fighting another faction.

11

Reptilian Propaganda
And The Dumbing Down Of Society

One of the best proofs that there is a reptilian agenda is inadvertently provided by the people who seek to ridicule, dismiss and debunk the topic. In this chapter we will study some of their writings. If, in the process, we discover techniques of manipulation and deceit, this really speaks for itself and supports the veracity of my claims.

The following is an article published by NBC news in 2020. The article is in italic writing, interspersed with my commentary in regular font.

Officials investigate whether Nashville bomber believed in 'lizard people'

The headline of this article already establishes, like so many other mainstream articles, that someone who believes in a reptilian agenda could be a terrorist. There are millions of peaceful, inquisitive people such as myself, who consider the possibility, but you'll find an inordinate amount of "news" items implying that reptilian researchers might somehow be *dangerous*. It's really simplistic propaganda.

WHAT DO YOU KNOW ABOUT HUMAN HARVESTING?

The world-ruled-by-lizard-people fantasy shot to prominence in recent years in part through the ramblings of David Icke, a popular British sports reporter-turned-conspiracy theorist known for his eccentric ideas.

From the outset there is no doubt that the topic of reptilians is fantasy, ramblings, conspiracy theory and eccentric. That's four words of defamation in only one sentence, as if to make very sure the whole concept is thoroughly shut down. There's not even the pretense of objectivity. The intent is not to examine the issue, but to belittle the people who believe in it.

Icke would have you believe that a race of reptilian beings not only invaded Earth, but that it also created a genetically modified lizard-human hybrid race called the "Babylonian Brotherhood," which, he maintains, is busy plotting a worldwide fascist state. This sinister cabal of global reptilian elites boasts a membership list including former President Barack Obama, Queen Elizabeth II of Great Britain, former Federal Reserve Chairman Alan Greenspan and Mick Jagger.

This nonsense is espoused by a variety of internet conspiracy-mongers, including far-right, Trump-loving QAnon adherents,

When propagandists lack facts to back up their assertions, they use insults. These are also called ad-hominem attacks. Thus, we are called conspiracy-mongers, far-right and Trump-loving (like that's supposed to be something bad). The term far-right is associated with jackboot-wearing, genocidal, tyrannical maniacs and is overused by these "journalists" as a tool of insult. So far, the entire article is very low on *actual information.*

Ad-hominem is a logical fallacy that attacks the person or character of a person rather than their position. My position is "Hey, look, a lot of people, since thousands of years, are talking about Reptilians, maybe there's something to it!" and someone says "You extremist! Terrorist!"

People who study journalism actually learn not to use ad-hominem because it casts a bad light on their work. The sheer amount of ad-hominem in this article reveals that the person writing it is not a journalist in the classical sense but a shill.

This is really good news for reptilian-researchers. If these people behaved like legitimate journalists and did a level-headed rebuttal of the reptilian theory, we'd be in trouble.

one of whom was accused in 2019 of murdering his own brother because he thought he was a lizard.

At the onset, reptilian researchers were linked to terrorists. Here they are linked to murderers. It really makes you wonder who writes this kind of stuff and who is paying them to write it.

As many as 12 million Americans believed in this lizard people conspiracy in a 2013 Public Policy Polling survey. It's safe to assume the number is higher today.

This nonsense is espoused by a variety of conspiracy-mongers, including one of whom was accused of murdering his own brother because he thought he was a lizard.

It is necessary to *again* remind the reader that these are conspiracy-mongers and potential murderers. That's really the central message of the article.

The outlandish trope has roots in the second half of the 19th century, when the Industrial Revolution, Darwin's theory of evolution and rapid scientific advances upended time-honored traditional ways of life, leaving people unsettled and unsure what to believe.

Here, reptilian researchers are linked to insecure and fearful people, another classical propaganda technique. Who would want to be part of that group? I fell for the propaganda when I was young, but it no longer works on me because I've seen these techniques used over and over on many topics related to the nefarious.

It emerged more strongly toward the end of the century, when anxieties about perceived outsiders, especially Jewish ones, were fueled by waves of immigrants flooding urban centers in Great Britain and the United States in search of economic prosperity and religious freedom. The tide of immigrants ignited cultural conflicts, as well as health and sanitation crises, in cities that lacked adequate infrastructure for the millions of arrivals.

Subtext: Reptilian researchers are anti-semites and racists. They are worried about immigrants. Can you believe the audacity of these writers? By now, your average person interested in the reptilian agenda is a murderer, terrorist, far-right extremist, insecure, fearful and anti-semite and god forbid, a Trump supporter!

Amid this tumult, a colorful array of gurus and charismatic figures arrived on the scene claiming secret knowledge of world affairs and answers to burning questions. The writings of the Russian-born mystic Helena Blavatsky, the founder of Theosophy, bristle with cosmic energies and mysterious knowledge — including her claim of an ancient race of dragon men from a lost continent mentioned in her esoteric 1888 tome, "The Secret Doctrine."

Source: https://www.nbcnews.com/think/opinion/qanon-s-capitol-rioters-nashville-bomber-s-lizard-people-theory-ncna1253819

The article goes on for a while in the same style, but it's not really worth our time.

If a mainstream article doesn't use rapid-fire ad-hominem, it uses tongue-in-cheek mockery. A few lines from an article in Vice Magazine, titled *Lizard people: the greatest political conspiracy ever created.*

Wait. People actually believe in this stuff?

Yes.

Is there any actual documentation of lizard people affecting the American government?

Nope, but sometimes lizard people make national news anyway

Am I a lizard person?

Possibly. Only you can know for sure. But hey, there are worse things you could be than a humanoid lizard with plans for world domination. That's pretty ambitious and admirable. Congratulations.

Source: https://www.vox.com/2014/11/5/7158371/lizard-people-conspiracy-theory-explainer

There are 12 million people in the U.S. who believe in reptilians (I believe the number to be much higher), but these "journalists" seem unable to address the issue with any sincerity except for childish ridicule and angry insult. A brief search on "reptilians" unveiled article after article in the same dumbed-down, insincere, jeering styles. I even found an article in the Atlantic Magazine (you know, the one run by a close friend of Ghislaine Maxwell), implying that reptilian researchers are mentally ill.

By pure logical deduction I have to conclude that the reptilian agenda is real. The reaction of a normal human being to millions of reports about reptilians and surely thousands of authors, would be to examine the claims, like I have in this book. The human reaction is to be open to both sides—could be true, could be wrong. Even after having researched, I'm still open to being proven wrong. For all I know, all the evidence on reptilians could have been planted. I don't believe that, but I'm always ready to learn more. That's sane human behavior.

But the propagandistic repetition of ad-hominem insults that are entirely unrelated to the topic—"racist!"—"anti-semite!"—"terrorist!"—"potential murderer!"—"conspiracy monger!"—"mentally ill!" and the jeering, are not normal human reactions to a topic of concern for so many people. I consider the reactions and methodology of the "debunkers" as the *strongest* proof for a reptilian agenda, because it's just so dumb and predictable. I could provide a much better debunk of reptilian-belief than that. A more subtle and intelligent one. These debunks are at grade-school level, for a gullible audience.

Don't allow them to shame you for questioning the state of the world. Noting that there are strange things happening and that elites collaborate to bring about mass-change, as in the 2020-22 fake covid "pandemic", does not make you a far-right fascist terrorist. It strikes me as strange to have to explain such a thing. Questioning authority is really the *opposite* of what they consider "far right fascist".

There is an entire Wikipedia page titled "Reptilian Conspiracy Theory". It teaches us little about reptilians and a lot about deceptive writing techniques. Quotes from the page, interspersed with my commentary:

Alien abduction narratives sometimes allege contact with reptilian creatures. One of the earliest reports was that of Ashland, Nebraska police officer Herbert Schirmer, who under hypnosis recalled being taken aboard a UFO in 1967 by humanoid beings with a slightly reptilian appearance, who wore a "winged serpent" emblem on the left side of their chests. Skeptics consider his claims to be a hoax.

This is the only alien abduction citation on the whole page. There is no mention of the fact that a large chunk, possibly 30% of abductee accounts mention reptiles or reptilians. That's tens of thousands of reports. The article cites one fairly unknown report and concludes with "Skeptics consider it to be a hoax".

The logical fallacy used here (that no serious, educated journalist is supposed to use) is the Strawman Fallacy. That's when you attack a distorted or weaker variation of the position rather than the position argued by most reptilian-agenda researchers.

Some adherents of the QAnon conspiracy theory have also borrowed from the reptilian conspiracy theory ,including elements shared in anti-Semitism conspiracy theories.

Almost every "debunking" I read seems to include some accusation of anti-semitism.

You've just read a book on reptilians—were Jews mentioned just once in this book? I don't even remember. Maybe they were, but never in a demeaning context. The "anti-semite" label is an overused attempt to shame people. An anti-semite, in their minds, is a potential mass-murderer, a genocidal, evil dictator.

It's true some think "the Jews" are an international cabal, a conspiracy to dominate the world and enslave the non-Jew cattle. What reptilian researchers are really saying is that it's not "Jews" pulling the strings but a non-human, extraterrestrial or subterranean, serpentine entity.

In reality, the continual use of the word anti-semite is creepy. I wish to say to the debunkers "We never mentioned Jews, why do you keep mentioning them?" Frankly, if I were a Jew, I wouldn't want the name of my people being invoked every time someone thinks a thought outside the mainstream. Reptilians is not the only topic in which Jews are invoked. According to mainstream media, you hate Jews (are an anti-semite) if you are skeptical of vaccines, if you think the federal reserve needs to be audited, if you are skeptical of the CIA and a long list of other things. Rarely does anyone ever ask "Dear Journalist—are you saying that vaccines, the federal reserve and the CIA are run by Jews?" The fact that the anti-semite card is drawn in each such instance, thousands of times over, is actually evidence that the reptilians wish to malign Jews. The Jews are blamed for every problem under the sun, to divert attention from the reptilian behind the curtain.

Historian Edward Guimont has argued that the reptilian conspiracy theory, particularly as expounded by Icke, drew from earlier pseudohistorical legends developed during the colonisation of Africa, particularly surrounding Great Zimbabwe and the mokele-mbembe.

Bizarrely, there is not a single mention, on the entire page, that the mythology of the Mayans, Egyptians, the shamans of ancient Russia, the Chinese, the Hindus, Buddhists, Christians, Islam, Judaism, the legends of the Aborigines of Australia, the Maori, the Pacific Islanders,

Africans, etc. contain hundreds of thousands of stories on reptilians. Let's just ignore that sheer wealth of ancient documentation and focus on only one mythological story from Zimbabwe, shall we? When I tried adding some of this data to the page, it was removed. I was told it belonged to mythology, not reptilians.

With this book, I have shared only about 1% of what I know about the dragon people. There is so much documentation and sincere research on the topic that I could fill a hundred more thick volumes on it. The way mainstream articles are written you quickly realize there is *no real interest* in learning anything about the topic—not even about why so many people believe in it, or why all ancient cultures knew about the serpent-people. Again, a genuine scientific stance would be "OK, we don't believe these fanciful stories, but what is it about the collective unconscious that makes people concerned about reptilians? Why do all the old cultures have similar sounding stories and recurring themes?"

If journalism, research, inquiry or investigation are not the goal here, then what is? It's attack.

Reptilian propaganda is not limited to debunking reptilians. One of my best pieces of evidence for the existence of an evil, human-hating cabal is the state of "journalism". Most people know that the presidential elections of 2020 were rigged. Even most opponents of that President know it. And yet, mainstream media, in unison, decries this statement as "the big lie" and has censored it across social media platforms. I've had two of my videos removed from YouTube for implying "election fraud". One more removal and YouTube will shut down my channel which I've spent 15 years building and cultivating. That means I have to now be careful of what I say, like in any other communist or fascist dictatorship.

This incident is only one in millions of daily instances of censorship by mass-media in conjunction with "big tech" companies in silicon valley, California.

Reptilian propaganda is not only falsehoods being told but *mainly* what is being omitted–the stuff you never get to see. A few years ago, I created the website titled falsehistory. net. Its articles can easily be found on lesser search engines but there is no trace of most articles on Google, at the time of this writing. Reptilian censorship is *hidden* censorship. In *open* censorship, which is vastly more integrous, I'd receive a notification telling me that my material has been banned and why. But the reptilian mindset is void of integrity. They shadowban material they don't like, hiding it without you ever knowing it's hidden. On top of that, they'll deny it's happening. This practice has resulted in numerous successful lawsuits against social media companies and search engines because there are mathematical and statistical ways to prove the insidious practice. Shadowbanning, a practice always denied by the social media company Twitter, turned out to be a reality in the 2023 Twitter-files scandal. As a result, the Twitter brand shut down, its architects were fired, and the brand renamed after a 2022 takeover by Elon Musk. Subsequently, the appearance was created that the new owners value "free speech" and no longer do shadow-banning. Whether that's true, remains to be seen at the time of this writing.

Even more shocking than tools of mass-censorship and reality-manipulation is the passive apathy of the general populace. The brands that censor, hide, lie and cheat, the ones that mine your data and spy on you, such as Gmail, to name one of many examples, continue to be the most popular, most used and most loved.

Why? How? One of the reasons has to do with familiarity-needs. Evildoers are expert at manipulating people's familiarity needs, as I've expounded on in other books. Gmail is familiar, so it "feels safe". "Everybody uses it, so I can gain acceptance in my community if I also use it". "Because I know it, it's easier to use and I don't have to invest attention using an unfamiliar program". So great is people's need for a "feeling of safety and familiarity" (not actual safety because Gmail is the least safe place to send, receive and store messages) that they are often puzzled when

I provide them email addresses of unknown domains. Some even ask "Don't you have a normal address, like Gmail?" Many even require such an address. There are also plenty of online platforms that can only be used if you "login with Facebook" or "login with Gmail". For instance, when I get a traffic ticket for speeding, something that happens to me about once a year, the only way to pay the ticket is by credit card or google pay. As I don't have a credit card, the only option to pay is to have a Google account. Why don't I have a credit card? Because I don't participate in the reptilian debt-slavery system. I do have a Google account without which I can't participate in many normal activities of daily life.

The fact that we, as a society, allow complete dependence on one company, is a sign of our dumbing down. Another great example is the site booking.com. I've noticed this one because I travel several times a year. Increasingly fewer Hotels are willing to take direct bookings. They direct me to the company booking.com. Even if I show up directly at the Hotel, asking for a room for the night, they say "Could you log in at booking.com? We can't really do anything from here". Another receptionist told me recently "You get a $100 discount if you do it at booking.com". I ask: Why are people so eager to give up their independence? Why is every Hotel I enter now beholden to one global company called booking.com?

One of the teachings of the reptilian-mindset is that "to succeed, you must compromise your integrity". In the last years I have cancelled several contracts and coaching-businesses with people and companies because their values represent a negative mindset. For instance, one company required that I take covid shots and boosters if I were to continue working with them. "Please inject these toxins, then you can have success with us". I categorically refused and "lost" the Business but really maintained my integrity.

Maintaining your integrity to a large extent, is of utmost importance in combating the reptilian mind. It's what *angers them the most* because it keeps your level of consciousness and energy out of their reach.

The great dumbing down of society is seen in every sector. Parents give their children "processed foods" (toxins) for "nourishment". Consequently, their children suffer ADHD, Dyslexia and other disorders. Instead of discontinuing the bad food, they then resort to equally toxic pharmaceuticals to "fix" the problem. The pharma addiction then causes other problems, which require even more pills to address, and so on. How dumb can you be and still breathe?

I could go on, dissecting every aspect of society, showing how it's been infiltrated by a non-loving, dumbed-down reptilian mindset. But just these few examples should suffice. Or not? No, unfortunately not.

A sign of intelligence is to extrapolate information. If I cite an example of reptilian infiltration in the medical industry, the smart reader will extrapolate and think "Hm–OK, how might this apply in the software industry?" or "What is the reptilian mindset in the military?" The great dumbing down could entail that people no longer extrapolate. "You didn't give any examples of the software industry, Fred, so I thought it's fine".

Here's a fact: The last three laptops with Windows operating system that I've purchased were manufactured by Asus, Lenovo and Toshiba. They were in the "high price" range. If you asked me which of these laptops is better, I couldn't tell you because they were almost exactly the same. I call this "fake choice" or "fake competition". As far as I can tell, each of these "brands" are made by the same people, otherwise you'd find the real difference.

The same goes for rental car companies: How do they differ from each other? Or airlines: What sets one airline apart from the other? The airlines within the U.S. are almost identical and equally low-quality. When I use an airline I am sent a long questionnaire in which I'm supposed to expound on how wonderful my "experience" with them was. But I fail to see what sets one airline apart from another. There are only a few airlines I've seen that are truly a class above the rest. The trend toward uniformity and blandness is of a reptilian mindset. The reason is that reptilians have a hive-mind in which uniqueness and individuality are not much valued. From this you could extrapolate that communism is a reptilian philosophy. You could extrapolate anything about everything if you were to regain the power to think for yourself.

Previously I've noted that society is experiencing a raise in levels of consciousness. How does that relate to the idea that society is actually dumbing down? Well, I call this "the great divergence". We are living in times where humanity is diverging, with one part more dull-minded than ever and another part more conscious than ever. Previously there was more of a middle ground where it could go both ways. People were "mixed bags". Today we have more "fully conscious" vs. "fully unconscious" people than before. It's more difficult to remain on neutral ground in light of various world events.

12

How Good People Can Take Back Companies From Psychopaths

In this chapter I show how organizations are penetrated and taken over by psychopaths and how integrous people can take them back. In terms of consciousness-levels, integrous means above level 300 and psychopath means below level 100.

The strength and weakness of Hierarchy

Most organizational charts end up in the shape of a Pyramid. At a lower to mid consciousness a sense of individuality is not yet developed, so people prefer joining a group and following a leader. The leader is part of another group that follows an even higher leader and so on. There is nothing good or bad about this, it's just part of human nature. The hierarchy structures' advantages: It provides order, orientation and more rapid decision-making for an organization. I am not against hierarchy and authority, but the system also has weaknesses. It's vulnerable to corruption. The larger the organization the more vulnerable, because the leader loses sight of all the individual parts. If it's a large Pyramid, the top has a hard time seeing the lower parts and usually only talks with the parts immediately below; having no first-hand experience of what's happening in the rest of the group.

The good, the bad and the normie

99% of people are neither entirely good nor entirely bad, they are a mix. Groups are the same way. People try to malign entire organizations but every social organism has good and less good people in it. Within a religious organization or a political party or a company you can have saintly people and psychopaths. Almost every company has a shadow, a suppressed subconscious, just like the individual. Releasing the shadow side requires for it to come to light. A group entirely run by psychopaths is a crime organization. A trick that professional criminals sometimes use is have the lower parts of the company run by *integrous people* as a *front or façade* to hide the non-integrous activities happening at the top. In my twenties there was a training institute that hired me as their face, a naïve and innocent guy to make the company look good. The leader of the company was later arrested for a long list of crimes I had no idea of. I thought he was "somehow creepy" but I used to suppress such thoughts as not to be judgmental. Later I learned difference between intuition and judgementalism.

Maybe you've heard the term "the good, the bad, the ugly". Another term is the sheep, the wolves and the sheepdog. The sheep or the ugly are also called normies or NPCs. These are people who don't have a focus, vision or values of their own and just *follow along* with whatever the crowd does. The only way our planet has a future is if we can stop calling the normies normies or even worse the ugly or even the sheep and *enlist them* to awaken. There are a lot of good people among so-called normies. It takes only one integrous person taking action to counterbalance the influence of 100 psychopaths. When good people stop sitting on the sidelines just observing and coasting along and instead ACT, world peace and abundance can happen overnight.

Small corruption

Every organization has people that don't behave in alignment with the group goals.

For example a low-level employee extracting small sums of money from the organization, too small for anyone to notice but adding up over the years. Instead of adding to the company, he acts as a parasite. I've indicated it in gray in this picture. Most large companies expect and account for such minor losses, knowing that not everyone is integrous and hoping that most people are helping the company.

A common mistake parasites make, is to keep signalling what they are adding to the company to compensate for the fact that they are subtracting. The smart don't tell you how smart they are, the rich don't tell you how rich they are, the tough don't tell you how tough they are, the honest don't tell you how honest they are. Only con artists do. So if you have someone who often signals how virtuous and integrous they are, how charitable, how socially conscious, how generous, etc. it could very well be an indicator of hidden corruption.

Let's say an integrous company opens up a branch in a corrupt country where there are already existing mafia-like structures. They wish to take a cut of whatever the company makes. If they can't gain access to the higher ups, they want to at least get to a low-level employee. They look for someone who is susceptible to bribery or corruption. They look for people in *desperate need* or the *aggressively ambitious*. If they can't find one who lacks integrity, they must threaten him or his family. People commit non-integrous acts out of greed or fear. This is how psychopaths first gain access. But long before that happens, the person they gain access to felt *isolated* from the companys goals and values and separated from the team. If the employee or worker were identified with the company or in good rapport with the team, it would be so much more difficult to solicit him for corrupt activities. *You only get attacked externally if you're already under attack internally.* Self-abuse comes before abuse from others. This image illustrates the point:

A strong family, company, humanity.

A weakened family, company, humanity.

Groups create such a dynamic that it's sometimes difficult to penetrate a positive team. They stick together and are averse to strangers. So the external psychopath needs to find a spot of vulnerability. Thus, family-run businesses are harder to penetrate because family usually has loyalty to each other. But in places in which everyone is *anonymous* to each other with nothing that bonds them or keeps them committed to each other, infiltration becomes easy. There are advantages to working from home, but lack of contact to your teammates is not a good thing for any group. The definition of a group is that they work together, not each for themselves.

Psychopaths of Everyday Life

Within Group dynamics it can be hard to stop psychopaths. I used to be a member of this group of about 50 people who met up to play Tennis. Among them was one person who always brought his boombox with obnoxious music. He cranked up the volume during the matches. Amazingly, nobody said anything, even though some were visibly annoyed. They gave him looks, whispered among each other but nobody asked him to quit. Why not? Because he had an aggressive demeanor.

Imposing on others while having *zero interest* in what they prefer, is the primary trait of a psychopath. The opposite - consideration of people–is a trait of integrous folks. When an entire group is scared to confront a person, it's because he or she has an "atmosphere" that induces fear. Sheep are terrified of confronting the wolf. So you need a sheepdog–a confident, integrous person.

What can a normie do in that situation? If you are scared of confronting the person, you can ask a higher up. Unless that person is also a psycho, they'll help. You might be shamed as a tattletale and nobody likes do-gooders who tell on others. That's how the psychopath would put it. But shaming you for standing up to them is just one of their many tools of oppression.

Because I want to transcend my own normie-ness, I usually try to *confront the person before* I report them to higher ups. It can be more difficult but it's more integrous to give them a chance to change.

After a few weeks of this, certainly a little late, I confronted him. His response proved him a psychopath. I politely asked "Could you please turn off your music? I don't want to listen to it and I wasn't asked". I wasn't playing on his tennis court but the music was so loud I couldn't hear the people I was playing with. Instead of turning it off, he addressed his co-players: "Are you guys bothered by the music? Anyone here bothered?" One person said "No, I'm OK with it". Another said "It's OK. I mean it doesn't bother me personally". And another just shrugged, apparently trying the "no opinion" or neutral option, which, when a psychopath is present is the same thing as agreeing with the psychopath. So he looked over at me and said "You see? That's democracy. The vote is for keeping the music".

What's really happening here is that the psychopath already has his own group hypnotized, so they won't contradict him. Nobody from my court or my group came to my assistance because they too are to some extent afraid of confrontation with him. The psychopath gave me a look like "how dare you question me, I'll deal with you later when nobody is watching". So the music kept playing.

At first sight it looked like everyone was in agreement with the psychopath, a consensus had been reached, democracy had been practiced. People can really make it look that way. You might start doubting your own sanity or integrity. For a moment I thought "Maybe I'm the grumpy person here. Maybe I'm in the wrong. Maybe I need to mind my own Business". Even so, it bothered me. After the match I went to the Club office and said "Is it really necessary that we have one person's loud music overshadow our Tennis matches?" I was then told that *many people* had complained about it. Many people! This means that the *appearance of a democratic consensus had been an illusion,* manufactured by the hypnotic, fear-inducing presence of the psychopath. It was good for me to hear that, realizing I'm not the lone truther. The higher ups told me that bringing your own music to tennis is "unacceptable". Promptly the guy was *removed from the club* and the organizations stated values and goals could be continued.

I once had a neighbor who never took her three dogs for a walk, which to me, amounts to animal abuse. She sometimes left her home for days and the dogs would be barking day and night. That's abuse of neighbors. I have a hard time intervening in other peoples' business because I believe we are each responsible for our own reality, so for some time I said nothing. But soon the situation descended below the threshold of acceptability with the dogs howling more painfully and frequently. People suggested I call animal rescue. But I first confronted the psychopath personally, writing her a letter about the problem. Writing to her instead of confronting her at the door would give her a chance to think about her response. The barking immediately stopped as she had someone stay at the house while she was gone. She also moved the dogs to another part of the house where we didn't even hear them much when they did bark.

The "abuse of neighbors" was solved, but she still wasn't taking the dogs for walks. Psychopaths often only do the very least they have to do to avoid being reported or being exposed. I moved away before reporting this and it's one of those things where, looking back, I should have reported. We have to weigh our aversion to meddling in other peoples' Business with doing what's right. As a general rule I'd never intervene unless a living being is being abused and in this case, it's reasonable to assume that living beings were being abused. Abuse and neglect is the way of the psychopath. Appreciation, Interest, Care and Conscientiousness is the way of the integrous person.

How to Spot an Integrous Person

There are telltale signs of integrous people too. But it's often not by what they display or show openly but how they act when nobody is watching. In one social experiment a wallet with money is left on the street. It contains the owners name and phone number visibly written on the wallet. 95% of people look around to check if they are being watched. If nobody is looking, they pocket the money. Only 5% contact the owner to return the money. Most people do the right thing because they fear consequences or due to peer pressure. Only 5% are at a consciousness level to be integrous regardless of who is watching. They understand that integrity is a powerful generator of abundance.

Global Levels of Integrity

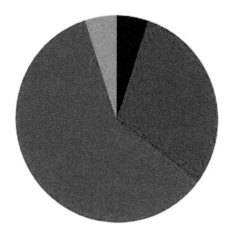

■ No Integrity (5%) ■ Some Integrity (30%)
■ Mostly Integrous (60%) ■ Total Integrity (5%)

How do employees act when the boss is absent? How do people act when no authority is around? When there are no laws? Do circumstances become chaotic quickly, like in "Mad Max" or do people stay civilized and responsible? Well, that depends on their level of consciousness.

If you yourself are integrous you easily spot and discern integrous vs. non-integrous people. You can see it in their soft eyes, their sense of humor, their compassion, their reaction to suffering, their level of attention, their sincerity.

High-Level Corruption

Those who wish to penetrate an organization normally don't aim for low-level positions. If the psychopath becomes head of department, then it's as if anyone below him were also corrupt because those below him are working for his ends. If those below him are making money, it *flows upwards* for the Head of Department to manage. And if he funnels it out of the company, you have *several lower employees working for corruption regardless of whether they know it*. From this you see not everyone in a company has to be corrupted, it's enough if the top is. That's why psychopaths target upper positions. And that's why you have somewhat more integrity among "normal folk" or at the bottom of the Pyramid.

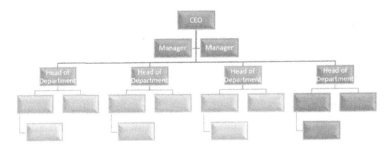

If you have a situation as in this image, an entire chunk of an organization has been corrupted and the employees below will soon come under the spell of a new culture or leave the department. People below the psychopath will gradually be replaced by people with little will or power of their own. Sycophants. It's interesting how similar the word *sycophant* and *psychopath* are, as they often arise together.

in spite of difficulty. That's the training, and that makes you so powerful. Despite all the problems you can still feel the love and come from the chest and treat your fellow humans with kindness.

Yes, there are agendas to harvest the energy of people, as I've explained this in my book *The Electromagnetic Self* and now in this book. But that's not the only game happening. The evil is like a small cup of water compared to the tsunami of goodness that is overwhelming the universe. If you have no access to that it's because you have disconnected yourself from intuition you have disconnected yourself from your conscience. People lose their conscience (the ability to discern good and bad) through their own negative conduct. They can get dulled to a point they no longer feel much, no longer know what to believe or trust no longer know what's real.

There is an effort in the world, to confuse people so they can no longer tell what's real. This agenda is delivered to you through the media. If you ever get confused as to what is true or false, switch off all media, become silent and look into your heart for answers.

People who haven't broken their intuition, discernment and conscience can tell true from false easily. It's not that difficult, as falsehood always has the same vibe, whether thousands of years ago or today. Confusion is a tool of falsehood. When you're in a confused mindset, you call good evil and evil good. But you have to look at the fruits of the thing, the overall results of a thing in order to understand whether something is good or not.

From what I can tell, energy is harvested from people on Earth and from people in the lower-astral and lower-to-mid-astral. It is not harvested in higher realms because there is an abundance of energy for all beings in those realms. You know this to be true because you, yourself, being an integrous person, probably don't engage in the exploitation and vampirism of other people and their energy. If you would never do that, why assume everyone else does? This goes back to my teaching of "the way you see the Universe, is the way you are". Your view of God has a lot to do with your view of yourself. If you've been abused all your life and have, consequently, started abusing others, all you see is abuse. So you develop a cosmology of abuse. But beyond all of our projections, there is a way of seeing the Universe as-it-is. Neither negatively nor positively filtered. And when you see it as it is, it's deliciously beautiful and fascinating, in spite of some of the dark spots.

Conclusion

I wrote this book to find satisfactory answers for myself. Is there a reptilian conspiracy? Or is "reptilian" only a metaphor? Are they spiritual or physical? And are there benevolent beings among them?

After spending a year in research, I am certain it's not a metaphor. The creatures are real spiritually and physically. The anti-human agenda has been obvious to me for a long time now, but after this book there is no doubt. I also know we are divinely created and more powerful than we know. I've glimpsed a higher meaning to all of this: It's a cosmic game of us testing our powers on a secretive and formidable adversary.

Are there "positive reptilians"? I guess so. There are always exceptions to the rule. As shown earlier, reptilians were created in a place called Heaven, as incredibly beautiful beings. The bible says that Lucifer was an anointed angel, and the most beautiful of God's creations.

Are there "positive entities"? Yes, there surely are. Can we enlist the positive ones to help overcome those who seek to oppress humanity? I don't know. I'm not a great believer in enlisting external help for something *we can do and should have already done of our own initiative*, long ago. I sense that this is one of our purposes for being here, a part of our cosmic script that has yet to manifest.

My four solutions–spiritual work, lawsuits, citizen journalism and small businesses are good advice for life regardless of whether one believes in reptilians. Even if you don't believe in them, surely you've noticed the dysfunctional aspects of society that need fixing? If so, contribute to the repair of the world. The slow and creeping process of enslavement can be reversed.

May you find lasting peace and prosperity,

Frederick Dodson

www.realitycreation.org

Books Referenced

A list of books referenced, by other authors. None of these books are recommended or endorsed, but do serve for further research.

David Icke / Children of the Matrix

William Bramley / Gods of Eden

Nick Redfern / Bloodline of the Gods

Credo Mutwa / The hidden History of Africa

Patricia Lynch / African Mythology from A to Z

Susan Reed / The Body Snatchers

Susan Reed / Conspiracy in the Heavens

A.P. Elkin / Aboriginal Men of High Degree

Kerth Barker / Blood-Drinking, Cannibalism and High-Adept Satanism

Eda Kalmre / The Human-Sausage Factory

Cathy O'Brien / Trance-formation of America

James Bartley / The Reptilian Mind

Scott M. Peck / People of the Lie

Carlos Castaneda / The Active Side of Infinity

Other books by the author can be found here:

www.realitycreation.org/books

Printed in Great Britain
by Amazon

40037547R00155